Contents

MARKETING

The Essential Guide

Antonia
Chitty &
Victoria
Dawson

Marketing – The Essential Guide is also available in accessible formats for people with any degree of visual impairment. The large print edition and eBook (with accessibility features enabled) are available from Need2Know. Please let us know if there are any special features you require and we will do our best to accommodate your needs.

First published in Great Britain in 2011 by
Need2Know
Remus House
Coltsfoot Drive
Peterborough
PE2 9BF
Telephone 01733 898103
Fax 01733 313524
www.need2knowbooks.co.uk

Introduction

There is a lot to learn when you start to market a business. Marketing covers an enormous range of activities, before you start to think about PR, sales and advertising. For any business owner or marketing manager, it is critical to your business's success that you have plenty of ideas for spreading the word about the company at your fingertips. Whether you are a sole trader and want to do your own marketing, or manage a small team and need to know more about the topic, this is the book for you. If you are a beginner, we start with marketing basics and introduce you to sales, PR and advertising too. Whether you're new to marketing or an experienced marketer, this book will bring you up to date on how to use social media for promotion.

In chapter 1, you can learn the critical elements to get right before doing any promotional activity. Find out how to create great branding for your company, using colours, words and logos. Establish your target audience, where to find them and how to communicate. Determine your business's unique selling points and understand how to set aims and goals for your marketing, the first steps to success.

Chapter 2 helps you take what you have learnt about your brand and put it into practice for marketing your business. You can find out more about understanding your customers' motivations, and be introduced to some of the elements of setting up your marketing campaign so that every activity you do builds on your work rather than happening in isolation. Learn basic sales strategies that tie in with marketing messages, and understand what a 'call to action' is and how it can work for you and your business to make your marketing help you achieve your goals. You'll also cover topics including product funnels, evaluating marketing and developing promotional materials that get results.

In chapter 3, we move slightly away from marketing to give you an introduction to PR. For anyone working in a small business, a knowledge of how to do your own PR can ensure that you really make the most of your marketing budget, reach potential customers via media that they trust, and back up paid advertising. You'll learn what makes news, and how to write, send and follow up your own press release. Don't ignore this chapter: PR is a great tool to use.

Similarly, in chapter 4 you can learn about sales and advertising. An effective marketing strategy will bring these different disciplines into play in a complementary manner. You can learn how to plan effective advertising, however small your budget. Plus, you get an introduction to a few key strategies used by successful sales people, discover the essentials for a sales pitch and understand the basics of cross selling, upselling and telesales amongst other concepts.

From chapter 5 onwards, we move to marketing online. No business can afford to ignore the enormous potential for marketing via the Internet. In this chapter we first address your own website, looking at site design, designers, hosting, plus the legal requirements for your site. In addition, we introduce you to the basics of search engine optimisation, or getting the search engines to help your potential customers find your products and services.

'No business can afford to ignore the enormous potential for marketing via the Internet.'

In chapter 6, we 'Start Marketing Online'. Learn about sales pages, squeeze pages, landing pages and conversion rates, all simple concepts to make your online marketing more effective. Discover how to build and market via an email list, creating newsletters and offers to your list by email. You'll also get a quick introduction to eCourses and eBooks to offer incentives and value to your potential customers.

Chapter 7 introduces you to social media for online promotion. Find out why Twitter is great news if you're promoting a business and how to move beyond a personal Facebook account and turn your Facebook 'page' into a vital tool for your business to reach new people. In Chapter 8 you can learn about blogs and why they are the new marketing essential. Get to grips with the practicalities of setting up a blog and using it for outreach and to build relationships with new and existing clients. We'll share key tips and tricks for getting readers to your blog, and then from your blog to buy from your business.

Finally, chapter 9 brings everything that you have learnt together with a focus on planning and evaluation. You can pull together what you have learnt from the first 8 chapters to create your own inspired plan for ongoing marketing and promotion, and you'll get an idea of how to tell what will work for your business. Discover how to pin down your objectives and which activities to plan in order to meet them. Also within this chapter you'll get an introduction to finding freelancers and commissioning agencies to back up your own in-house expertise.

By the end of this book you should be full of ideas and ready to start marketing your business successfully.

Chapter One

Introduction to Marketing

Marketing covers an enormous range of activities, and for any business owner it is critical to your business's success. Whether you are a sole trader and want to do your own marketing, or manage a small team and need to know more about the topic, read on.

In this chapter we introduce you to some essential marketing basics that will help you clarify your ideas about your own business and ensure that any marketing you do is as effective as possible.

Why promote your business?

As a business owner, you might feel that your main aim in life is to run your business, to create the products or offer the services you provide, and marketing can feel like a secondary activity. For real business success, however, put marketing at the top of the list of all your business activities. Marketing is all about communicating what your business offers to the right people. What is more, your marketing activities should look at solving their problems and creating regular communications so you can develop a relationship with these people. Very little marketing is about the hard sell – much more it is about ensuring that, when anyone needs to buy a service or product that you offer, it is your business that they think of first.

In this book we won't just be talking about marketing in the abstract. Every marketing concept we touch upon will have direct relevance to your business. We'll be asking you to look at your business and think how to apply the concept, then giving you practical tips on how to do so. Early on in the book you need to work out your specific goals for your business overall, and for your marketing activity in particular, so that every marketing activity you do can take you closer to achieving these goals.

'Marketing is all about communicating what your business offers to the right people.'

Numbers count

Do you know how many new people you will have to show your business offer to before one of them bites? You may need to reach as many as 1,000 new people before you get a sale. You can learn two things from this. Firstly, do everything you can to spread the word about your business. Use online and offline techniques and don't rule out any marketing tool until you have tried it. Secondly, find some way of collating your contacts, either in your own database or on something like Constant Contact, Profollow or Aweber. That will help you try out new and successful marketing ideas.

Marketing 101

How much do you know about marketing? Whether you are a total beginner or need to brush up your skills, here are some important ideas to think about.

Your brand

Every business has a brand, and as part of your marketing strategy you need to look at your brand, consider what it represents and think about the values people learn about your business from the brand.

Practically, your brand can be represented by your business name, certain images, colours and words. Your business brand will help people identify and remember your business. On a deeper level, though, what are you trying to get people to understand about your business? A brand should sum up everything a consumer could find valuable about your company.

Think about the products you buy from the supermarket each week. Which products are you happy to buy 'own brand' versions of and which do you want a specific brand? If you always want a particular brand of bread or beans, why do you make this choice? And then think about this in the wider world. Why do different groups of people shop at certain stores? What different brand qualities do you perceive between Marks & Spencers, Boden or New Look? Would you opt for a Skoda, a Renault or a Lamborghini?

The three Cs of branding

When Dee Blick, author of *Powerful Marketing On A Shoestring Budget For Small Businesses*, began her marketing career 26 years ago she thought that branding was purely about logos. Now, she explains, 'Although important, there's more to branding than just looks. So, before considering how you can build your small business into a brand contemplate this definition of branding from Philip Kotler, a world expert on the subject:

"A brand is a promise to your customers, the totality of perceptions about a product, service or business, the relationship customers have with it based on past experiences, present associations and future expectations. Brand reality is always defined by the customer's view".

'It is what your customer thinks about your brand, not what you think that will ultimately determine its long-term success.

How can you apply Kotler's definition to your business? Start by focusing on the 3 Cs of branding:

- Consistency
- Clarity
- Continuity

'Successful brands are consistent. This means that when customers or prospects engage with your business, they benefit from the same consistent treatment each time. To attain a high level of consistency, you must identify each contact point and look at how it can be improved from your customers' perspective.

'Successful brands are clear in the messages they deliver. They know exactly what they stand for, exactly why customers buy from them and why they continue to buy. They don't overcomplicate their core messages and they always look at their business through the eyes of their customers when developing their benefit statements.

'Successful brands are in it for the long haul. Customers need reassuring that the businesses they do business with will be around for many years to come. Are you investing in your business to build strong and sustainable foundations and communicating this?

'If you can commit to an annual brand audit encompassing the 3 Cs, you'll never be at risk of complacency.'

'Although important, there's more to branding than just looks.'
Dee Blick.

Thinking about your own business, what values would you like people to know it for? Ask your clients or customers to talk about the company and how they perceive it. Then see whether the two match up. As part of your marketing you need to move consumers' views towards the brand identity that you want to create.

Logo

A logo is the first thing many people consider when looking at a company's branding. Alongside the business name, the visual image is helpful in creating instant recognition amongst potential and existing customers. It can help you create international recognition beyond words.

Your choice of colours for your logo can play a key factor in how your business is perceived. Different colours stimulate and reflect different emotions. Different densities of colour can alter the emotions generated – compare how you feel in a pastel room to one with bright toned walls and furnishings. Different cultures will have different associations with particular colours.

- Pink: youth, for girls, fun, frivolous.
- Red: fast, hot, love, blood.
- Orange: happiness, warmth.
- Yellow: bright, wellbeing, cheerful.
- Green: natural, healthy, eco-friendly.
- Blue: calm, clean, fresh.
- Black: modern, intense, youth, death (in Western cultures), serious.
- Grey: serious, businesslike, dull.
- White: marriage (in Western cultures), death (in Eastern cultures).

Think of three logos that stand out to you and note down the companies associated with them, download images or sketch what you remember of the logo. Look at them and ask yourself, what makes them stand out to you? How has the designer used colour, shapes and even lettering to come up with the logo. What values do these other companies put across through their logos? And then investigate each of the three businesses to see where they use their logo. How does this assist their brand image and marketing?

Now, look at the logo for your business. Where do consumers see your logo? Is it conveying the message that you want? Get your logo right and include it with your marketing to build your brand presence throughout your marketing. Read the sections below about strapline, target audience and unique selling point too, as this will help you refine your logo and decide what it needs to put across to people who see it.

Need to create a new logo?

Gather other images which you think reflect values you want to put across for your business. You might be attracted to images of flowers if you want to portray a business that is 'fresh', for example. Look at your selection of images and write down the words that come to mind. Don't censor yourself: just jot down the first words that come to mind. Circle 1, 2 or 3 of those words which you'd like people to use when describing your business. Then, ask yourself which colours convey these values best.

Now you have some ideas for words, colours and images which describe your business. Think about where you will use any branding: does it have to fit on product packaging, head up a website or be used on promotional materials? If you have a good idea about where you'll need to use your branding you can note down the different versions which you might need.

At this point, you may want to hand over a list of your ideas and requirements to a graphic designer to build into a brand image for you. Designers will usually create a range of options for you to choose from. Alternatively, you may want to start sketching out some ideas yourself, either by hand or using a graphic design programme. Test out your ideas on people who fit your target audience before finalising them.

'Think of three logos that stand out to you and note down the companies associated with them – ask yourself, what makes them stand out to you?'

Strapline

Alongside your logo you may want to use a strapline for your business. If your business name does *not* make it clear what you offer, a strapline is essential. Until your business reaches the size of Coca-Cola, Amazon or Disney, you need to spell out to people how you can help them. This applies if you have an acronym for your main trading name, or a person's name or a made-up word.

If your business has a descriptive name, such as 'John's Computer Repairs', you may decide that the business name sums up your offer already, but a strapline can also explain about the quality of your services or products. It can emphasise what you offer over and above other competing businesses. It needs to be concise and memorable.

If 'John's Computer Repairs' wanted to develop a strapline, it could cover the business's key promise of a speedy repair and highlight that the business focuses on PCs rather than Macs: 'John's Computer Repairs – Your PC Fixed Fast'.

What sort of name does your business have? Does it tell people what you offer, or do you need to explain? Are there key qualities to your business that you need to emphasise in the strapline? If you have a strapline already, what does it tell customers? Does it back up the brand identity you are developing? Decide if you need to create a new strapline for your business.

Target audience

When you are creating a logo, strapline and brand, you need to be clear about who your target audience is. What groups does your business provide services or products for? If you are unclear about this it makes it far harder to target any marketing activities, as different groups respond in different ways to messages, and can be reached by different marketing methods and activities.

You may have a database of customer details already which can tell you who is buying what, where they live, what they spend and much more (demographics). If you don't have this sort of database already, start to gather basic demographic detail about the people who buy from your business. You need to know their age, address, sex, and you might want to consider if there are other relevant lifestyle factors e.g. do your customers tend to be new parents, parents to teens, childless, single/married etc. There will be demographics that are particularly relevant to your type of business.

If you don't have a database, or feel that you don't really know your target customer, you may want to survey your potential market. Use a service like www.surveymonkey.com to develop an online survey. Remember that some people are more likely to fill in a paper survey, so purely running an online survey could bias your responses. Think about which method is most likely to reach your potential customers or whether you should use both printed and online surveys. You could also look at contracting a company to carry out a survey for you, if you have a budget of a few thousand pounds.

In your survey, ask respondents what they read/watch, where they go, and where they might look for information on your product or service. Find out about their income bands and shopping habits too. Ask about their buying habits, to provide facts about who might buy from you and what they are looking for. Drill down to explore their need for your product or service and possible frequency of purchase.

'What makes your business's offering special and different?'

When you have your survey results, use them to draw up a picture of your main target audience. You might find it useful to use images to illustrate the sort of person you are targeting. You may find that you have a range of different groups to target with different products. Are there some people who come to your business for free advice or just to browse? What makes them different to those who buy occasionally and those who are frequent and regular customers? If you can begin to understand who are your best customers, you can focus your marketing activities to find more of these people, and achieve the best return for your efforts.

Unique selling point (USP)

What makes your business's offering special and different? Unless you are clear about this you can't market effectively. If you know and understand the specific benefits that your company offers, and how they differ to the competition's products or services, you are in a much better position to share this with your target audience. These specific benefits can be known as your company's unique selling point (USP).

If you are not clear, why not gather some material to help develop your USP? Chat to colleagues and ask them how they see your enterprise standing out from others. More importantly, ask your customers and clients why they come to you. The unique perceived benefit (UPB) for your business looks at how your customer feels they benefit from your offer, rather than the USP which is traditionally created from the company's perspective.

Once you understand what is unique and different about your business, consider how you will integrate this into your marketing messages. Bear your USP – or UPB – in mind throughout the following chapters and as you plan your marketing campaigns.

Elevator pitch

If you know your business's USP/UPB, now is the time to develop your elevator pitch. This is a short talk which outlines your business benefits to a potential contact in around 30 seconds, approximately the time it takes to go up in a lift! Once you can explain your unique proposition succinctly and clearly like this, you are well placed to develop all sorts of marketing ideas. As a marketer, you'll need a range of snappy ways to write about your business offer as well as being able to pitch verbally. Plan what you want to say now, and you'll have the material ready as you develop your marketing activities.

Clear on your concepts?

Take time to go through your branding, logo and strapline, your USP and elevator pitch and to develop your knowledge about your target audience. It is well worth getting these marketing basics right before you attempt to market your business.

Setting your goals for business promotion

As well as being clear about how you want your business to come across, you also need to be clear about your aims for your business overall, and also for your marketing.

Aims

Think about the aim for your business. This is a broad outline of what you want the business to do. Why did you set it up, and what might you want the business to achieve in the next five or 10 years? Write down a paragraph describing this. Alternatively, you may be the sort of person who is inspired by a great vision for your business: would you find it helpful to describe how the business will be in the future in words, or would it motivate you more to create a vision board using images of where you want the business to be in a few years time? Then, look at breaking your aim down into objectives.

Objectives

An objective is a measurable step that will make progress towards your overall aim. You will probably need a handful of goals to work towards, with some short-term, some medium-term and some longer-term ones. Depending on how your mind works, it can help you achieve if your goals are SMART – Specific, Measurable, Achievable, Realistic and Time-specific.

For your business you will probably need to develop (or have developed already) objectives for specific areas. You should have financial targets, sales targets, and, most relevant to this book, targets for your marketing activities.

Think about the number of objectives that are achievable over a certain time period. You might like to develop three to four goals for the short, medium and long-term – to achieve in the next few months, the next couple of years and over 5-10 years perhaps. Don't feel that you have to have four in each time period: equally, feel free to add in further goals if relevant to you and your business.

Your early goals may simply include to create a marketing plan – always a good place to start (and there's more about this towards the end of the book). Then, start looking at your financial targets: how much does your business need to sell in order to reach these targets? And once you know the sales targets, consider how many people you might need to reach in order to make that many sales – this is where the initial marketing goals come in. You can set goals to reach, and also goals for conversion – how many of the people you reach who actually go on to buy.

On a personal level, you may choose a goal such as trying a marketing activity that is new to you each month or quarter: this is an ideal way to continually extend your marketing reach and see what works best. Or, you might focus on one way of marketing that you know works well for your business and see if you can apply it to more people or improve the way you do it to lead to more sales.

Whatever you want to achieve, take a moment now to focus on your own goals and the goals for your business as this will help you make the most of what you learn from this book.

Persistence – key to marketing

'People need up to seven opportunities to view your message before they take action.'

People need up to seven opportunities to view your message before they take action. Most businesses do not get the response they hope for the very first time they carry out most marketing activities. If the people you are contacting have not come across your business before, you are likely to need to contact them several times before getting results. Allow time and money for repeat marketing activities to make the most of your initial investment.

Summing Up

In this chapter you have been introduced to some key ideas in marketing. Are you now clear about your branding, logo and strapline, your USP and elevator pitch? Do you understand your target audience, who they are and why and when they might buy from you? It is well worth getting these marketing basics right before you attempt to market your business.

Additionally, are you clear about your aims for your business? Where does it need to be this time next year, in five years' time and in ten years' time? And have you got the objectives in place to give you a clear route to achieving your aims? Invest time in getting this right *now* and it will ensure that your marketing efforts drive your business in the direction you need.

There are hundreds of ways to market and more than one will be right for your business: read on throughout this book and you'll get an introduction to some new ideas to help you. If you feel that marketing hasn't worked for you in the past, you just haven't found the right way to reach your particular customer group. Keep trying out new marketing ideas. Go to chapter 2 to find out more about branding and practical guidance on how using your branding and developing a range of promotional materials can help you reach your target audience.

Quick action checklist:

- Set goals for your business.

- Look at your business brand – do you need to create or update your logo or strapline?

- What do you know about your target audience? Do you need to do a survey?

- Are you clear about what's unique about your business and why your customers come to you? Write down your USP/UPBs.

- Make a quick list of the four main ways that you have found contacts, clients or customers so far: this will help you in chapters to come.

Chapter Two

Turn Branding into Business

In chapter 1 you read all about developing your business brand. Are you now clear about your branding, logo and strapline, your USP and elevator pitch? Do you understand your target audience, who they are and why and when they might buy from you? Have you got some clear goals for your business in mind? In this chapter we look at developing your understanding of branding and putting together some essential business tools to get your marketing off to a great start.

Brand building - the basics of marketing

The aim of building your business brand is all about ensuring that people come to you before your competitors. You need to make sure that potential customers are not just aware of your logo and strapline, but also of the values behind them.

How does your business communicate?

Marketing is all about communication, and the way your business communicates affects how people perceive it. If you have a clear coherent message couched on language that is right for your target audience they will start to take on board what you say. If your messages are muddled or delivered in a way that irritates your potential customers, your marketing communications can harm your business. Think carefully about the frequency and volume of communications with your potential and existing customers, and remember to read the section on page 78, about the legalities of marketing communications too.

How do people in your business behave?

The people within your business also have a great impact on how your business, and your brand, is perceived. If you have staff who know and understand your latest marketing initiatives they will be better able to respond in a helpful way to enquirers. On a very simple level, you wouldn't send out a catalogue with a new special offer without checking that you had the stock in place and the staff ready to pick, pack and dispatch the surge of orders you were hoping to generate. In the same way, if you are creating a new marketing campaign to highlight the swift service your business offers, you need to make sure that every member of staff is aware of the 24-hour delivery guarantee on the flyers. This book does not go into internal communications, but communicating with your staff is every bit as important as communicating with the outside world. The way each customer is greeted, every order dealt with and every phone call answered contributes to the perception of your business brand and to your business's success.

'Marketing should not be about continually giving people the message you want them to hear: instead it needs to be about building a relationship with them.'

Build relationships through marketing

Marketing should not be about continually giving people the message you want them to hear: instead it needs to be about building a relationship with them so that they understand the unique benefits that your business offers and how it can solve their particular problems. Marketing communications need to be developed strategically: think of the action you want people to take at the end of the process and all the ways you might persuade them that taking that action will benefit them. Then use those ideas to develop your marketing campaign.

Understanding your customers

The best way to understand what will motivate someone to buy, is to ask them. You may want to gather a small group of people together to discuss your business – a focus group. A focus group involves around eight people who are asked questions on a topic then allowed to discuss this with relatively free reign. You'll need to create a topic guide to take the group through the areas you want to cover, and to record the group as it takes place so you can listen back to what they discuss. The discussion should last around an hour to two hours, depending on the complexity of the topic you are discussing. You should offer attendees some sort of incentive or recompense for their time.

You may only have time or budget to run a single group, but it is best practice to run three or more focus groups. Because of the person-led nature of the discussion format, you may find that a single group's views are swayed by its members and not necessarily representative of all your target audience. If you run three groups you can see which trends appear across all three, and which issues are only raised by one of the groups.

Recruit people from a relevant group of your target audience. If your business targets men and women aged 25-44, you might have a focus group made up of people within this group. You could, however, split your groups so that you have a group of around eight men and a group of a similar number of women, and you may get different views from each group. You would need to run three groups for each gender, though, before you could start to say that women respond differently to your brand to men.

There are short courses to train you to run focus groups.

Seven touches

It makes sense that, the more a potential customer sees your business, the more likely they are to buy. As long as you have coherent and positive branding and promotional messages, this cumulative effect will see wavering consumers turn into buyers. It is amazing, then, that so many business owners are disappointed when a single advert or marketing activity fails to realise the results they hoped for.

The idea of contacting a potential buyer seven times is a long-standing marketing basic, and if you are planning any sort of marketing, you'll need to build this into your plans. Add up advertising, public relations leading to media coverage, online promotion and direct sales, as well as many other techniques that you'll learn about in this book in order to ensure that your target audience gets as many chances to view your message as possible.

More ways to 'touch':

- A visit to your website.
- An email.
- A phone call.
- A recommendation by word of mouth.
- A newsletter.
- Meeting one of your team at a network event.
- A face to face meeting.
- An advert.

Remember that not everyone will see every marketing activity that you do, and you'll begin to understand why just one, two or even three promotions may not get the results you need. Instead, ongoing regular promotion, focused on your target audience throughout the year is the best way to get results. Have a plan that you continually update, ways to evaluate what is working, and systems to make sure that enquiries are followed up. Depending on your business, you should look at making sure your marketing activities link smoothly with your sales team: they may provide the vital telephone or face-to-face contact that will convert someone who knows and likes your business into a purchaser.

Your business follow-up system

This is an example of one way that a business promotes it services.

- Find a potential new contact at a networking event.
- Send them an email the day after the event.
- Add them to the mailing list – remember to select focused areas of interest, or invite them to do so themselves.
- Send regular newsletters once a week or once a month.
- Offer a free report.
- Send a free report.

- Follow up with a phone call asking about their views on the report and how you can help them.

- Build up to a face-to-face meeting.

What system do you need to develop for *your* business?

Of course, 'seven touches' is not going to be true every time. If you get your marketing messages just right, you may convert people to buy with your first contact. Nonetheless, having regular adverts, media coverage, email and postal communications with your prospects, is the way to build relationships and ensure that people:

- Trust your business.

- Know what you offer.

- Understand the benefits.

- And choose *your business* when they need to buy.

Some marketers have estimated it can take as many as 30 touches to convince someone to buy: does this help you see why your marketing efforts need to be comprehensive, planned and ongoing?

Cold contacts? Warm them up!

People who haven't heard about your business yet are 'cold contacts': those who have signed up for your newsletter, sent an enquiry, or purchased from you are 'warm'. It is much easier to get warm contacts to buy again than to get cold contacts to buy, and much more cost-effective too, so make sure you nurture your current contacts and customers with ongoing marketing.

Making real contact

Within any communication to potential customers and clients you need to engage with the person in order to market to them. An American sales pioneer, E. St. Elmo Lewis is responsible for a model that has lasted over 100 years, with some adaptation, to explain how to engage. He suggested that successful sales people used strategies to lead people through four levels of interest in a product or service, with the acronym AIDA. The target person's thought processes move through:

- Attention (also can be known as Awareness): the first step to attracting someone.
- Interest: where benefits of the product or service are demonstrated and made relevant to the target.
- Desire: convincing the person that they need and want what is on offer.
- Action: taking the action that the salesperson is leading them to.

You can also add in Satisfaction, the stage at which customers are happy with what they have purchased and can be encouraged to make repeat purchases and make referrals. Other variations include:

- AIDPPC: description instead of Desire, followed by Persuasion, Proof and Close.
- AIDCA: inserting Conviction between Desire and Action.

Your call to action

Throughout all of your marketing you need a clear 'call to action'. A call to action is simply what you want the reader or viewer to do once they have seen (or even heard) your marketing message. If you are clear about your business aims and targets (see chapter 1) it makes it much easier to develop your calls to action. You are likely to need different calls to action for different marketing 'campaigns' and throughout each campaign you may build up to a call to action – or you may make it explicit right from the start.

Simple 'calls to action':

- Call this number 0800 123 4567...

- Phone 0800 XXX XXX now.

- Visit www.yourbusiness.co.uk to find out more.

- Sign up at www.yourbusiness.co.uk/offer to get your discount voucher.

- Sign up for your newsletter here.

- Send off this coupon for your free sample.

- Add to cart.

Calls to action are short and clear and you need to be extremely clear about what action you want people to take to ensure that they are clear too. In online promotion your call to action is likely to have a clickable link behind the text so people are taken smoothly through, perhaps to the page where they can buy the product you are promoting. *Always* make sure that there is a *single* call to action at the end of your marketing communications: don't give multiple choices. You may want to give people reminders about the call to action throughout the text of a communication.

When developing a marketing campaign, you may want to have a cascade of calls to action that draw people further in. As one example, here is a simple online marketing campaign:

- A blog post which invites readers to 'sign up for the newsletter and get a discount voucher'.

- A newsletter with the voucher and some useful information for people to read which takes them into your website.

- A follow-up email which showcases some products they might spend the voucher on and asks them to 'buy now'.

As part of your call to action you can also include the benefit or reason why they need to take the particular action. Again, keep this very short and focused – sometimes the benefit is simply something *free*! Remember to create this from the point of view of the potential customer. Put yourself in their shoes and ask 'what's in it for me?'. You might also consider making it clear if any offer is time-limited as this can focus people's minds.

'A call to action is simply what you want the reader or viewer to do once they have seen your marketing message.'

What's a marketing campaign?

If you are marketing a business, you may have ongoing activities to raise the general business profile, but you will also have specific 'marketing campaigns'. A campaign will focus on one product, a new service, or even an action you want people to take. The campaign could have its own visual identity and theme and a plan of activities over a fixed timescale. It will have a strategic plan, which has been researched and is well thought out. It will use a range of activities which could include advertising, direct marketing, media work and online promotion, as well as personal appearances, endorsements, sampling events and more. It will have a specific budget and outcomes will look at sales of the product or service plus awareness raised.

Your products and marketing

Another important element to look at as part of your marketing is your product funnel. This is most easily understood visually: look at the diagram on the next page and ask yourself if you have something to offer people at a range of levels. If you have some free or very low cost items to offer you can use this to draw in people to share their details with your business. You can then start communicating your marketing messages to them, build a relationship and draw them further down the funnel. Many people will only commit to a small purchase, so have a range of products that are easily reproduced or bought in which you can encourage as many people as possible to buy. Then, look at how you might move this group of purchasers on to making bigger, more valuable buys. They are 'warm' to your business already so you need to look at how you can exploit your relationship and provide something that will 'solve their problems' even more effectively. Finally, you need your most valuable products, which only a few people in your funnel will go on to buy.

Something *free* or very low cost to entice people
to share their details with you

Something of moderate value that is
available to many

A product of higher value

Your highest value
products

Example 1: A product-based business – Sarah's Gift Shop

A discount voucher (which requires people to sign up on Sarah's
website or fill in their details on the reverse of the voucher).

A low cost gift or treat for the person to buy for themselves – small
cosmetics, affordable jewellery, little ornaments which Sarah
puts by the counter in her shop and suggests at checkout
on her website with the phrase 'treat yourself'.

A product of higher value that might be a gift or
special occasion treat: a glamorous handbag,
more expensive jewellery, gift sets of
cosmetics and toiletries.

Sarah's range of personalised
and customised high value
products and
gift boxes.

Example 2: A service-based business – Clive's Life Coaching

A free report on 7 ways to be happy: sign up on Clive's website to get this.

An eBook on developing happiness which Clive has written. It costs $9 and can be paid for and downloaded instantly from his site.

Group teleclasses where Clive offers a 1 hour training session on his secrets of happiness and the chance to ask questions. Up to 12 people can take part paying $97 each.

One-to-one session with Clive costing $297.

Clive's business as a coach could depend on the hours he has available, but by filling his product funnel he can increase his income *and* provide a range of ways to draw in more people who might not initially go for his 'big ticket' one-to-one coaching. In this way, a product funnel makes it easier to market his business across the globe – anyone can get his free report, pay a few dollars for his eBook or sign up for a teleclass – and draw people down to find the few who want, will value, and can pay for one-to-one work.

Think about your company product funnel – is it complete or are there noticeable gaps?

Can you count where your customers come from?

One simple but crucial bit of preparation which you need to do before you start marketing is to devise a way to see whether your marketing is working. The key to making the best use of your resources for promoting your business is to understand what gets results. And the only way to know what works is to ask your customers one simple question. Build 'Where did you hear of us?' into your online order form and newsletter sign-up forms and you will know where to invest your time and resources for maximum results. If your shopping cart can't do this, see if you can add a message to a simple autoresponder asking this question. If you have a bricks and mortar store, do you have a customer management system that can collect this data? Or simply put a notepad next to the till and jot down people's responses.

Start doing this *now* and you will be able to see which marketing methods are helping your business as you progress through this book and try out different marketing activities and tools.

Promotional materials

If you ask most people about marketing, they will talk to you about flyers and other printed materials. As you read through this book you'll see that there is much more to marketing than this, but equally it is important to get the basic marketing materials for your business right.

First, consider the materials that are used every day within your business. Do your headed notepaper and compliments slips put across the image that you want to create of your business? If customers and potential clients get a letter from you, is it instantly recognisable? Does it reinforce your current marketing campaign or back up your brand values? And when you and your colleagues attend networking and business meetings, do you have business cards and flyers to hand out that you are proud of, or do you apologetically explain that you need to get them updated?

Make a list of the regular materials that are used and give them a quick overhaul using the tips overleaf.

Marketing materials basics

To make sure your materials are a good investment, here are some simple tips:

- Have a clear call to action.
- Use larger print and fewer words.
- Cut back on adjectives and stick to facts.
- Get help with design to make your materials visually striking.
- Work out your distribution *before* you order.
- Choose a time period over which you want to use the materials, and consider when you might want to update your branding, strapline or other marketing messages.
- Order the number you know you can distribute plus around 10%.

You can apply these tips to all sorts of materials. Think about which of the following might help you promote your business:

- Flyers.
- Postcards.
- Brochures and catalogues.
- Direct mail.
- Sales letters.
- Printed enclosures.
- Promotional items – pens, mugs etc.
- Headed paper.
- Compliments slips.
- Business cards.

Summing Up

In this chapter you have learnt about how you can go from having an idea of your business brand to starting to develop some ideas about marketing the business. Are you now clear about:

▨ How you might begin to understand your target audience better?

▨ Why you need to repeat your key messages to get people to act?

▨ The need for a clear system to follow up warm leads?

▨ What is a 'call to action' and the basics of creating one?

▨ How to look at your business offering in terms of a 'product funnel'?

These basics will help you get your marketing right. Re-read the chapter if you are unclear, or move on to your action points.

Quick action checklist:

▨ Do you need to understand your target audience better? Think about holding a focus group.

▨ Start a notebook or file to plan your marketing. Gather together information about key events and launches for your company in the coming year.

▨ Liaise with your sales team about how they follow up leads and see how this fits with your marketing. If you don't have a sales team or a system, think about how you will follow up leads.

▨ Consider what you want your customers to do when you contact them. Can you ask them to 'buy now' straight away? What other 'calls to action' are relevant to your business and marketing campaign ideas?

▨ Look at your business offering in terms of a 'product funnel'. Do you have free, low cost, moderate cost and high cost items? What might you need to do to fill in any gaps?

Chapter Three

Effective Press Releases

Press releases can be an extremely useful way of marketing your business. They can be submitted to newspapers, magazines, radio and television stations to promote your business. In this chapter you will be shown how to write a newsworthy press release, how to develop relevant contacts with journalists and how to distribute your press release effectively. Remember to include press releases and public relations activity in your marketing plan.

Why use press releases?

Journalists are always on the lookout for stories. Press releases are the standard format used for businesses to communicate any newsworthy information to the media. Press releases can result in free publicity for your business, publicity that you simply could not afford to buy. The best publicity for your business tends to be free publicity.

Press releases can be used for virtually any type of business; if you aren't using press releases then you are missing out on one of the quickest and most cost-effective ways of promotion. You can pay for a company to write your press releases or you may wish to follow the guide in this chapter and have a go at writing your own. Press releases can now be sent out electronically, saving on postage costs.

When released online, press releases can also help with your SEO (search engine optimisation). A well-formatted press release will include keywords about your business and will be picked up by search engines if released online which can dramatically increase your web presence.

'The best publicity for your business tends to be free publicity.'

Newsworthy stories

Before starting to write a press release you need to think carefully about the content. Remember, journalists receive hundreds of press releases each week so you need to make sure that yours stands out.

Research your target audience

Consider whether you are going to aim your press release at the local press or national press. Buy copies of the papers and magazines that you hope that your press release will be featured in. Make a note of what businesses are being covered, what the stories are about. Cut out any items of interest and ask yourself:

- What is the main point of the story?
- Who is the story aimed at?
- Why has this story been covered?
- Who has written the story?

With this information in mind, you can review your own ideas for press releases and decide whether you think they would be appropriate for the publications.

Ideas for press releases

Every business has newsworthy stories connected to it. Set aside some time to consider what you could write about that is interesting. In this section you will find some ideas to begin with.

If you are introducing any new products or services, you can focus on how these will benefit readers through a press release. Make sure that you target your press release to reach your potential customers; for example if your product is aimed at mums you should consider which publications they will read.

Launching a new business can be of interest to local media. You could also send out a press release if you launch a new website or open a new office or store. Have you employed a new member of staff? Or have any of your staff achieved any awards? The press release can focus on how the member of staff's qualification can help the customer and will also help to create a professional image of your company.

If your business supports a local charity, let people know. This could be sponsoring a local sports team or organising fundraising events like a member of staff having their head shaved. Local media are usually very interested in covering stories around community service. Are you holding a special event, such as offering free talks in the community? If you have an insulation business you may want to offer free talks about how to keep warm in the winter, or a security business may wish to offer free talks about how to keep your home safer. Whatever you decide to do, make sure the local press know about it.

Current affairs can sometimes tie in well with your product or service. For example, if there is a news story about the dangers of tanning and you own a beauty salon you could send out a release about the benefits of spray tanning. Make sure that you listen to the news daily and if any relevant story breaks immediately send out a response.

Competitions are a great way to get some publicity for your business. Send out a press release to raise awareness of the competition and then another to announce the winner.

If anything unusual has happened around your business then let the press know. Have you had an exceptionally large order? Or have your staff been able to help in the community during adverse weather conditions? People are interested in reading about unusual happenings.

Make sure that your press releases are interesting and don't use technical jargon in them. If a press release is boring it is not likely to be used, read through your idea several times and consider whether others would find the content interesting.

Market research

Conduct some market research to find out what your customers think about your products and release the findings in a press release.

Does your story grab attention?

All press releases need to have a 'hook' or something that will appeal to the editors. Your press release must grab people's attention if it is going to have a good chance of being used. The first sentence of the press release is particularly important and needs to sum up the story for the reader while capturing their attention. Use a headline that will grab the reader's attention. Make sure that you are focusing on solving a problem for the reader.

'The first sentence of the press release is particularly important and needs to sum up the story for the reader while capturing their attention.'

The first paragraph of a press release should be about answering questions like:

- Who?
- Why?
- Where?
- What?
- When?
- How?

If the reader stops reading after the first paragraph they will have a good idea of the story. If you aren't sure about your press release, try it out on colleagues or contacts first for some honest feedback.

```
┌─────────────────────────────────────────────┐
│                                             │
│         ┌──────────────────────┐            │
│         │                      │            │
│         │      Your Logo       │            │
│         │                      │            │
│         └──────────────────────┘            │
│                                             │
```

Press Release

Issued Date _____ For Immediate Release

OR Embargoed Until Date _____

Title... make it brief and attention-grabbing

The first sentence should be a summary of the story. Get your key points across to catch the journalist's attention or they may not read further. Answer all the important questions like who, what, where, when, why and how. Write as if you are speaking to the readers of the publication – review your target publication for an appropriate style.

Expand on the details in the second paragraph. Remember the journalist will want to know what is unique or new about your story and why it will appeal to their readers. Then, back up your claims with facts and statistics in the following paragraphs. Write in the present tense, and use 'he' or 'she' instead of 'I'.

Go on to illustrate your story with quotes, "*A quote, written in italics, from a key person, helps bring a story to life. Make sure your quote adds new information to the release*".

As well as quotes, you could use bullet points to highlight points about your story:

• Special
• Timely
• Unique

Finish off with details such as dates, times, how to order or contact you – this only needs to be brief, and should be the details you would like to see in print. Fuller details can go in 'Notes to Editors'.

> It's simple to add a photo or illustration to catch the journalist's eye and bring the press release to life. If you are emailing it, make sure you use a low resolution image, so the file isn't too large.

##Ends##

This template was reproduced with kind permission from Antonia Chitty and is also available as a download from www.prbasics.co.uk

Top tips for writing your press release

Once you start writing press releases on a regular basis you will quickly learn the dos and don'ts. Here are some top tips to follow to make your press release professional:

- Keep press releases to one or two sides of A4.

- Double line spacing should be used so that there is space for editors to make notes.

- Use a clear font such as Ariel and preferably at least 12 point size.

- Align text to the left.

- Use your logo.

- Keep paragraphs short.

- If posting the release, produce it on a letterhead and number your pages.

- If your release is more than one page write 'more' at the bottom.

- Research the style of the publication and write in that style. Write in the present tense, writing in the past tense makes it sound like old news.

- Use facts rather than adjectives.

- Finish the release with ###ENDS### and always include a word count.

Notes to editors

At the end of your press release you should include a 'Notes to Editors' section. This is where you should place your contact number, company address, company name, website, email and fax number. It is useful to include when you are available to speak to the media and an after hours number if you can. You may also state whether you have photographs available to support your press release. You could also include a short section giving background information about your company such as when it was launched and any significant achievements.

Using photographs or images

Editors may want you to supply photographs to accompany your press release and good quality images can guarantee great coverage whereas poor images may lead to a story being dropped. You may also find that an image on a press release can help to draw attention to your news. Suppliers may be able to provide you with product shots if you sell their goods. If you make your own products you will need to provide your own photographs.

Build up a list of freelance photographers who will take photographs for your business. If you are looking to keep costs down you might find a photography student by contacting your local college.

If your business offers a service, finding suitable photographs can be more challenging. You could photograph people using your service with their consent or ask for a quote from one of them and perhaps include their photograph in your press release.

A program such as Adobe Photoshop Elements can help you to manipulate and improve your images. You can change your backgrounds, airbrush the image or add watermarks to them to prevent them being used by others.

Image quality

It is important that you are able to provide digital images to journalists either via email or on a disc. Initial and sample images can be of relatively low quality resolution; about 72 dots per inch (dpi) or pixels per inch (ppi). This will help to keep the file size or email size down; large files can take a long time to upload. Digital images for printing however need to be 'high resolution' with a minimum of 300 dpi. The dpi indicates how many dots per inch appear in each section of the image. The more dots per inch, the greater the detail and the clearer the image.

To find the resolution of an image you should right click on it and select 'properties'. The number of dpi is dependent on the size of the image. You may have a photo which is 300 dpi but only 2cm wide which will look very blurred if printed as a 5cm image. For print purposes you should aim for images that are 300 to 500 dpi and at least 10cm wide and high: some publications may want even larger images, so always ensure your photographer supplies images at high resolution.

Always begin with a high resolution image, you can reduce the quality to a low resolution image, but you cannot improve the quality of a low resolution image to a high one.

Sending your press release

You need to decide how you are going to distribute your press release. You can either send it by post or by email. You may wish to speak to the editor and ask whether they prefer to receive press releases on paper or electronically.

If you choose to send your press release by post you can see exactly how it will be presented to the journalist. You can be confident that the print quality is good, the colours are accurate and that the paper is of a high quality. If you wish to send the journalist a sample of your product then it is essential to send it alongside a printed press release.

If your press release covers more than one page, make sure that you number them and staple pages together. Label samples and images with your company name and contact details.

Many publications are now IT dependent and prefer to receive press releases via email. You should always paste the press release into the body of your email, never send as an attachment. To see how it looks, try sending it to yourself first. Avoid 'cc'ing people when sending press releases, it makes the email seem less personal.

Distribution sites

There are a number of organisations that are set up to distribute press releases for you. Some of these are free while others charge a fee. It is worth trying them to find out which may suit you and your business. Simply Google 'press release distribution sites' to find a range.

Journalists subscribe to the following sites to pick up news:

▓ www.responsesource.com

▓ www.journalism.co.uk

The following sites send press releases on your behalf charging to distribute the release that you have written:

- www.prnewswire.co.uk
- http://uk.cision.com/

Press packs

Press packs are a great way to get your business noticed by journalists. They comprise of a small folder including your press release plus any additional samples, photographs and information. You can be creative about what you send to the journalists and think about how you can get your press pack to stand out. Journalists are interested in anything that is different, so this is your chance to capture their attention. If you are on a small budget, carefully select a couple of publications that you would really like your product to be featured in. Call them up first to find out the right person to send the pack to.

You could include items in your press pack such as a business card, flyer or a catalogue. Write tip sheets or short articles to include. You may wish to include a CD of images for the journalist to use and a copy of your press release. Depending on what your business is you could include a sample of your product particularly if it is something like cake or chocolate. Some press packs even include a small gift for the journalist.

'Press packs are a great way to get your business noticed by journalists.'

Contacts

It is important to begin to make a database of contacts to send your press releases to. You could start with local media. Find out the names of all the local papers, radio stations and television stations. You should then get a specific name to send your press release to. Press releases that are addressed to an individual are more likely to get attention than those sent out randomly.

To find out who to send your press release to you should contact the organisation. Ask the editorial assistant or receptionist for the name of the person who handles the relevant pages or section of the publication. Record this information in your contact database.

You can create a contact database in a number of ways depending on your preference. A program such as Excel is an ideal way of keeping this information on file, or your business may have its own contact management system.

The table opposite gives you an idea of the sort of information that you will find useful to record. Use the blanks to have a go at starting your own database.

Resources to use

You may wish to use some of the following resources to help you to make your contact database. *The Writers' & Artists' Year Book* includes a range of contacts which are updated annually. This can be a good starting point for finding numbers to call for up-to-date named contacts. Your local library may have a copy in the reference section.

Other companies offer a subscription service usually costing several hundred pounds a month in exchange for thousands of UK media contacts which you can access online.

Making calls

Contacting journalists by telephone is a highly effective means of communication. It is much more personal than sending an email and makes you harder to ignore. Make a call before you send a press release. Set aside time to make calls so that you can give them your full attention

Follow these tips to make a good impression when you call:

- Plan your call, think about what you want to say.
- Write down your key points to remind you to get them across.
- Smile while you are speaking to them, it will come across at the other end of the line and will give you a more positive, confident aura.
- Use the journalist's name, it makes the call more personal.
- Ask them if it is a good time to chat, if not ask them when you should call back.
- Ask what sort of stories they are looking for.
- Tell them what you can offer them.
- If you can't offer them anything appropriate then suggest that you will get in touch when you have something relevant for them.

44

Organisation	Title	Contact name	Email	Address	Phone No	Comments	Press release sent
Sheffield Post	Assistant Editor	June Rose	June.rose@sheffieldpost.co.uk	12 Leopold St, Sheffield	0114 250572	Weekly paper goes to print Weds	Sent on 9th Sept. Follow up call 10th Sept, no answer to try again
Radio South	Producer	Ross Jenkins	Rossjenkins@radiosouth.com	15 High St, Camden	07977 287387	Breakfast show producer, wants guests to discuss current affairs	Sent on 18th August, appeared on radio show on 23rd August

Once you have established who to send the press release to you can forward it before making a follow-up call. Make sure that you have a good introductory sentence for your follow-up call, for example, 'My name is Alison and I'm calling from Divine Cakes. I sent you a press release yesterday about our new range of cup cakes for Valentine's Day.' You should then check if it is a good time for the journalist to talk.

When you have finished making a call, write any relevant comments into your database. Any actions should then be taken as soon as possible, so if you have said that you will send out a sample you should do this straight away.

'Radio stations are often interested in press releases and are frequently looking for experts in a wide variety of areas to contribute to their chat shows.'

Local media

Local media is a great way to get coverage for your business. There is less competition than with national press. Look in your local newspapers and list the staff's names and addresses. As suggested, give them a call and find out who covers stories most appropriate to your business. Aim to build a personal relationship with the staff, invite them to any product launches, send them samples and keep in touch with them on a regular basis. Find out if the paper has lifestyle supplements or a weekly review section that you could contribute to. To find out which papers cover your area search the databases at www. newspapersoc.org.uk

Radio

Radio stations are often interested in press releases and are frequently looking for experts in a wide variety of areas to contribute to their chat shows. If appearing on the radio seems a little daunting, just think about the amount of exposure it can create for your business. Research your local radio stations and listen to the programmes that they produce. This will give you an idea of the kind of topics that are discussed.

Contact each programme's forward planning team with your idea and availability. Use a 'Forward Planning Notice' which works for radio and for TV news shows and chat programmes.

FORWARD PLANNING / MEDIA NOTICE
INTERVIEW OPPORTUNITY
Business Mum Week: 2 – 10 October 2010

New book of proven business ideas paves the way to
success for millions of aspiring mumpreneurs

Background	Business Mum Week highlights the work and celebrates the success of our nation's mums who work from home, juggling family life. 76% of British mums who don't work for themselves would like to do so. A recent survey shows the majority of them are unable or unwilling to turn it into reality. Successful mumpreneurs Antonia Chitty and Helen Lindop have written an empowering, hands-on book, released to coincide with Business Mum Week: "Start a Family-Friendly Business: 23 brilliant business ideas for mums"
Interviewees	Antonia Chitty, mumpreneur and flexible-working expert
Availability	From Monday 04 October 2010
Contact	Lesley Singleton, LS Media, lesley@lsmedia. co.uk / 07852 451 093 / 01234 752 663

Business Mum Week is a key time for many aspiring mumpreneurs – the
children have gone back to school, and many mums' flexible working ideas
and business dreams start to take shape. But still, millions are held back,
daunted because they lack reliable information and insights about the
experience of launching and operating a business successfully.

LS Media Ltd
Company Registration No: 05831081
Registered Office: Suite 22 Savant House, 63-65 Camden High Street, London NW1 7JL

Packed with practical advice to help budding mumpreneurs launch the business that's right for them, "Start a Family-Friendly Business: 23 brilliant business ideas for mums" features over 120 proven ideas for flexible work and goes in-depth with 23 of them. Covering businesses as diverse as life coaching, childcare, personal training, cleaning, graphic design and journalism, the book outlines the pros and cons to give readers a detailed and realistic basis for decision-making.

"We wanted to share our real-life experience with mums who'd like to get started with their own business," says co-author, Antonia Chitty. "The 23 business ideas we've focused on are tried, tested and achievable. Using the information Helen and I share in the book, mums can work out which business would work for them, playing to their skills and strengths as well as fitting in with the demands of family life."

The book also includes no-nonsense tips to help mums take the first step on the road to successful self-employment, ranging from advice about business planning and complying with legislation to finding help with marketing and promotion.

"Start a Family-Friendly business: 23 brilliant ideas for business mums" is on sale from 15 September 2010. If you want to get your hands on a copy visit www.familyfriendlyworking.co.uk to pre-order, or buy online or in selected book stores including http://www.amazon.co.uk.

-ends-

For further information and to arrange an interview with Antonia Chitty, please contact

Lesley Singleton at LS Media on 01234 752 663 / 07852 451 093 or email Lesley@lsmedia.co.uk.

* The survey of 1000 mothers with children under the age of 18 in the UK was conducted in March 2010 by Redshift Research and social network MumsLikeYou for Phoenix Trading.

LS Media Ltd
Company Registration No: 05831081
Registered Office: Suite 22 Savant House, 63-65 Camden High Street, London NW1 7JL

If you do send your press release to a radio station and they invite you to talk on-air, follow these tips for a successful interview:

- Before the interview, ask the producer what the programme is going to be about and what they hope your contribution will be.

- You may be able to ask for the opening question too.

- Take some deep breaths and treat the interview as if it is just you and the presenter having a conversation.

- Smile, it will help you to feel more relaxed and you will sound confident.

- Write down three main points that you want to get across during the interview.

- Avoid using jargon, try to keep your points clear and concise.

- Make sure you say your company name and your website address at least once during the interview.

- If you don't know the answer to a question, explain that this is outside your remit but you would be interested in finding out the answer if any of the listeners know.

- Thank the presenter for their time.

Summing Up

In this chapter you have been introduced to press releases and how to use them effectively to promote your business. Do you feel that you can have a go at writing a press release? Do you understand what makes a press release newsworthy? It is well worth practising writing press releases and initially sending them out to the local media is a great way of getting started.

You have also been introduced to the importance of keeping a database of contacts. Are you more confident about telephoning journalists? Do you have an introduction to begin the phone call with? And are you listing your aims for the conversation so that you keep on track? Making sure that your press release is going to the right named contact will ensure that it is more likely to go to print and get your business the publicity that you desire.

There are many different subjects that you can write a press release about. If you haven't been successful with sending press releases in the past perhaps you can review whether your stories were newsworthy. Try out new ideas for press releases, writing about market research or tying in a press release to a particular season, for example, if you sell double glazing writing about winter approaching.

And if writing and sending press releases isn't for you, look for freelance or agency help. There's more on this in chapter 9.

There is much more to public relations that can be covered in one chapter, so continue to read and research on new ways to use PR to promote your business.

Quick action checklist:

- Identify a newsworthy story for a press release.
- Use the template on page 39 to write your own press release
- Build up a list of contacts using your database.
- Telephone your contacts and find out who to send the press release to.
- Send out your press release and follow this up with a phone call.

Chapter Four

Sales and Advertising

This chapter helps you see how advertising and sales need to fit into your marketing plan. Alongside public relations, which we looked at in the previous chapter, these elements traditionally completed your marketing strategy.

Advertising

Advertising is everywhere. On any journey you will pass advertising hoardings and billboards, see adverts in shop windows and in the free paper you pick up. At home adverts reach you through TV and radio, online and in print media as well as through your letterbox. In this chapter we look at how you can use advertising to complement your marketing strategy and make it stand out from the crowd.

'Advertising is everywhere.'

Focused advertising

Small businesses often struggle with advertising due to lack of planning. Here are a few tips to help you. Be clear about the profile of your potential customers – their age, income, location and habits. In chapter 1 you looked at who your target audience might be, and in chapter 2 you learnt a little about how to use surveys and focus groups to understand them more. Now you can put that knowledge to useful effect. Create a clear brief for the type(s) of person you want to reach with your advertising. This would include as much as you can about their age, marital and family status, location, income and habits. Then make a long list of possible advertising outlets, both on and offline. Buy the publications and/or check the websites for contacts and call the advertising departments to ask for their media packs. Check which publications' readers match the people you are trying to reach and you are on your first step to creating a focussed and effective advertising campaign.

Your customer profile:

Age	
Gender	
Location	
Marital status	
Family?	
Income bands	
Where they eat out	
What they read	
What they watch	
What they listen to	
Groups/clubs they belong to	
Your ideas . . .	

What's your budget?

Once you have your media packs you can also clarify your advertising budget and what it will get you. Your advertising budget may need to last the whole year through. You may decide that it is going to be more effective to have bursts of advertising at key points in the year for your business when people's minds are already on the problems that you could solve for them. Have you noticed how many more adverts there are for gifts in the run-up to Christmas? Which seasons are your busiest – would advertising in the run-up to these seasons complement your marketing and help drive sales?

With your headline figure in mind, look at the different combinations of advertising it could get for you. Would you want one or two full page ads in glossy magazines, backed up by ongoing smaller ads all year round? Or do you feel your money is better invested in lots of smaller advertisements online, all bringing customers direct to your website 24-7?

Designing effective adverts

Before getting into the copy and design of your advert, think about your objectives. What do you want your next advert to achieve? Take five minutes to note down *one* objective for your next advert. Try to be as detailed as possible: will it attract x enquiries or generate y sales over a certain time period?

I want my next advert to: ....

In your initial brief for your advertisement, explain how your product or service will benefit the buyer, rather than describing how many bells and whistles it comes with. It's much easier to sell a solution to a problem or a 'feel good' dream to someone this way. Use your advert to sell 'a better way of life for you and your family' rather than just promoting a business opportunity, for example.

Be clear what one call to action will form the basis of your advertising campaign. Put together some ideas for calls to action to get people reading an advert to take the action that would meet your objective. This could be as simple as 'get in touch' or 'buy this product now', but try making it specific to your business:

My call to action is: ....

How does this back up the rest of your marketing activities? Remember that people need to see a clear message up to seven times before they take action (see chapter 2), and your efforts will be more effective if they see the same message across your marketing and advertising, on and offline. Always back up print advertising by aiming PR at the same publications and consider offering a competition too for a further reminder about your offering to the readers.

Think about the content of your advert. Remember that a wordy advert can mean that readers miss the call to action. What images can embody your business offer and reinforce the call to action? Go back to chapter 1 and look at the information on colours. What emotions are you trying to get readers to feel? Can you use colour to achieve this? How will this drive them to take the action indicated on the advert? A designer should come up with three or more different advertising concepts which you can try out on focus groups to see the response each engenders. You can have different calls to action on the same designs and test these out to see how the response varies, either by using research or by actually placing the adverts and measuring responses.

Placing your ad

Once you have found out the sort of media that your potential customer reads by asking for media packs and designed and tested your advertisements you need to place your adverts. At an early stage it is wise to contact ad departments for their rates and find the deadlines for submitting artwork. There is little point in planning a great campaign if you don't have the space booked in your key publications.

Cost-saving tips:

■ *Do* have a list of key publications and websites that you'd like to advertise in.

■ *Don't* book an advert just because the sales person has called you and offered a great discount. If the publication isn't on your list it is unlikely to bring great dividends.

'One advert is not going to bring your business hundreds of customers.'

■ *Do* book if one of your key publications calls up with a great discount. Ad sales teams often call potential advertisers because they have space to fill and are under pressure to sell it so you can get the best price this way.

■ *Do* have your ad artwork ready as this will help if you are trying to get a last minute discount.

■ *Do* negotiate a discount for booking a series of ads.

Advertising troubleshooting

I often hear small business owners cry, 'I advertised but no one responded'. If you want to avoid this situation bear in mind:

■ It will take more than one advert. One advert is not going to bring your business hundreds of customers. It can take seven views of your message before a potential customer buys, so use repeat advertising that people will see on a number of occasions, in various publications or on repeat visits to websites and back this up with PR and marketing.

- Less is usually more. Focus on the one main outcome you want from your advert. Include a simple call to action like 'buy now' rather than trying to get every advantage of your product in one place. Cut out long descriptions and go for short punchy words.

- See it right. Make sure that your advert is visually striking. Use a freelance professional designer if you don't have great design skills in house, as this will make your investment in advertising more effective.

Planning your advertising

Think about the following sorts of advertising. Which might work well for your business? Mark the ones you need to investigate and build them into your marketing plan:

- Classified adverts.
- Directory advertising.
- Display adverts – national and local, magazines and newspapers.
- Vehicle advertising
- Radio advertising.
- TV advertising
- Internet banner advertising.
- Internet text link advertising.
- Adwords – pay per click.
- Advertising hoardings and posters.
- Cinema advertising.
- Direct mail.

Choose one sort of advertising that is new to your business. Investigate the costs and whether it will reach your target audience. Make a decision on whether this sort of advertising is going to benefit your business.

Sales

Does your business have a sales team? Whether you have lots of people out there directly selling to customers or you are a one person business with a website, there are lots of sales techniques that can help you.

How to sell

Selling is an issue faced by many business owners. You create a business that you love, offering a great service, or sharing your invention with friends who can't wait to try it out. You have an enormous amount of passion for your business – but don't see yourself as a salesperson. Yet selling is key to business success. Most of the time making a sale is about developing a relationship rather than flogging goods.

Relationship building – key to sales

If you approach someone who has never heard of you or your business and try to persuade them to buy, you might have an uphill struggle. If, however, someone is in touch with you on a regular basis, they will come to you to buy when they know that you have the products or services that they need at that particular point in time. So, for successful sales, you need to gather as many people as possible who have potential interest in your business and develop your relationship with them. For an online business the classic way to do this is to offer something free, yet valuable, in return for a person sharing their contact details with you. You could offer a discount voucher or a special report with expert advice. For a bricks and mortar store you may want a sign up book or postcards to fill in at the cash desk.

Once you have started gathering contact details, build ways to stay in touch with your customers. A short weekly email with one point of focus is probably better than a long complex newsletter that you can only produce every few months. Aim to offer regular news, tips and advice. People will come to value your communications and you can put in a more 'sales-y' approach every third newsletter, aiming to convert people to buy. Plus, your sales team will have a warmer welcome when they approach people who are well aware of your business already.

Read more about this in chapter 6

What's your problem?

When you are selling your products and services you shouldn't talk about what you do. Instead, focus on their needs. Ask your customers about the problems they experience and explain the solutions you offer. Get in touch with the emotions that you want your customer to feel. A mother buying a baby carrier is more likely to be persuaded if you tell her how babies who are carried are happy than if you point out the ways that the carrier ties. Think about how this might alter your 'sales pitch'.

Marketing basics: What's a sales pitch?

A sales pitch is a planned way to communicate the benefits of your offering to your potential customer. Your sales pitch could be used in a scripted telephone call or in a face-to-face meeting with or without visual materials to support the pitch.

Your sales pitch needs to allow you to understand the potential customer's motivation, be clear about how you could solve their problem, share the benefits, listen to their objections, overcome the objections and bring the sale to a close.

Asking questions to sell

You or your sales team need to practise using questions to both understand your prospect's needs *and* to bring them to the point of making a purchase.

Ways to close

There are a number of ways to close a sale – here are some ideas:

Assume the customer is going to buy. For example, by asking, 'How would you like to pay?'

Ask for the order. For example, 'Can I get you to sign here to confirm your order.'

'When you are selling your products and services you shouldn't talk about what you do. Instead, focus on their needs.'

Offer an either/or choice. For example, 'Would you like to order it in large or medium?'

Meet a customer demand. For example, 'So you'd like to place an order if we can . . .'

Make a list of positives and negatives and turn each negative round. For example, 'Yes, I can see this is more expensive than the competition, but based on the amount of wear you will get from it, it is much better value.'

More ways to sell

There are lots of techniques that can help you keep sales coming into your business. Think about how your business uses different sales techniques on an everyday basis. And make sales promotions part of your marketing plan, backed up by your marketing, PR and advertising.

Sales promotions

Use sales and discounts with caution: if you are perpetually offering discounts you will attract only those who are after something free or cheap. On the other hand, a sales promotion can encourage existing customers to try something new, extra or different. It can draw in new customers *and* at the same time allow you to shift stock that isn't moving as fast as you want.

Develop a plan for sales promotions. You could have quarterly sales on certain ranges or just sales in January and July across your products. And think smart: you don't just need to offer money off but you could make a sales promotion to encourage people to buy more. Tie this in with your marketing plan for maximum effect.

Cross-selling and upselling

Cross selling can help you make the most of your customers. When someone has just made a purchase they are very open to your business: suggest another product that they may like and they may well add it to their basket. Look at how Amazon does this the next time you make a purchase. Upselling is similar, and looks at how you can boost the value of what each customer buys by offering a slightly better option: like when you ask for a burger and end up buying a meal. Consider how this additional product or upgrade will meet what the customer needs: you know about what they need from their first purchase. Make your recommendation once the first product is in the customer's basket, and highlight special offers, discounts and bulk buy offers. Again, look at Amazon. You click to buy book A, they swiftly point out that you'll save if you buy book A and book B together, and book B is likely to be something that appeals to someone who chooses book A.

Think about how cross-selling and/or upselling might work within your business. Look at your shopping cart to see if you can make automatic suggestions, or adapt your 'thank you' page or email replies to make further relevant offers to shoppers. In a bricks and mortar store, think about what you can say to customers at point of sale to encourage them to add something. And watch how other businesses do this too.

Ideas for your sales promotions

Could you:

- Include a free sample of something new with every order for a limited period?

- Create a bundle offer – buy item A and we'll include item B for half the usual price?

- Use supermarket tactics: buy one get one free etc?

Spend some time this week looking at what other businesses offer as sales promotions. Which ones might help your business? Make a plan and schedule in when you will implement each sales promotion.

Telesales

Telesales is an area where many business owners lack confidence. A phone call can market your business, though, in a way that an email can't. You can ensure that your messages get to the right person and rapidly adapt your approach and response to what their individual needs are. There are a number of tools that make telemarketing easier:

- Contacts databases – do you have a list of potential people to call? Who follows up people who have enquired by phone or email? How might you gather a database of contacts?

- Call scripts – it is easier to be a confident sales person and get the right results if you have a tried and tested script. There are professionals who can create a script for you. Don't feel you have to read it out – a natural practised approach works much better. Do have a list of frequently asked questions to guide your sales people.

- Divide your contacts into warm and cold: you may need a different approach for people who you are contacting for the first time. People who have made an enquiry, even if they have not yet bought, are likely to be warmer to your approach. Previous customers are the most likely to buy.

'A phone call can market your business in a way that an email can't.'

Look at how you use the phone in your business. Do you have a database of enquirers and customers *with* phone numbers? If not, start collecting numbers. If you have people's numbers, think about why you might call them. What benefit could you offer them, and what action would you want them to take? Develop a script with some possible ways a conversation could pan out. Look at the information in 'Ways to close' and try them – on a friend or colleague at first if you haven't made business calls like this before. Then start slotting in some time to follow up clients or call enquirers each week.

Summing Up

Advertising can work for any business, but only if it is well designed, in the right place, and backed up by other marketing and PR. Make sure that you understand your target audience and how to reach them. Check out different advertising outlets, on and offline. Gather together media packs and rate cards to inform your decisions, so you are sure that you are placing adverts in media viewed by your target audience. Use negotiating skills and good timing to get the best price possible for your advertising campaigns.

Sales are essential for your business to succeed. Make them part of your marketing plan, and ensure that advertising, PR and other activities all tie into your sales promotions. Build relationships with people before selling to them: people who are warm to your business are far more likely to buy than cold contacts who have never heard of it before. As you get to know your potential customers you will better understand their problems and how you can showcase your business benefits to solve them. Think about your sales promotions and consider whether you could add in cross-selling and upselling to improve the amount people spend when they buy from you. And consider telesales as a great way to develop relationships as well as to sell your products or services.

If you need to know more about sales and advertising, start by researching different topics online, buying books and investigating professional bodies specific to these topics.

Quick action checklist:

▪ Find out about the sort of customer you want to reach.

▪ Call for media packs.

▪ Work on your advertising budget.

▪ Develop a clear call to action for your advert.

▪ Book ads and negotiate discounts.

▪ Look at how your business sells right now.

▪ Develop a list of people to call.

- Create a telesales script.
- Schedule in time to make calls every week if you don't have a sales team.
- Look at other techniques for selling and add them to your business.

Chapter Five

Online Promotion

With more and more people accessing the Internet, online promotion can be a great way to promote your business. In this chapter you will learn how a successful website will help to market your business 24 hours a day and seven days a week. A well produced website can help you get ahead of your competitors and market your business to more potential customers.

Why have a website?

If you don't already have a website for your business, you may feel that it isn't particularly important. A website is, however, a powerful marketing tool for any business.

Advantages of having a website:

- Your business is promoted while you sleep.
- Your website is always accessible: potential clients can read about your business outside office hours.
- You can update a website so that the latest news about your business is always on display.
- Your website will build your corporate brand.
- Nowadays a website can instill confidence in potential customers who might not buy if you can't be found online. A website will help you to compete with businesses who are already online.
- Your business will reach a wider audience nationally and globally.
- Selling online can cut down or spread the overheads of owning a shop.

- Many customers enjoy browsing a website before making a decision about buying goods or services.

- You can use a website to advertise for staff, inform customers of news and advertise new products or services.

- Fresh articles on your website keep you in touch with your target audience.

Having read the list of advantages, consider how your business would benefit from having a website.

Website design

'Remember, your website will showcase your business and it is essential that it looks good so that it markets your organisation effectively.'

It is important that you take some time to think about what sort of website is right for your business. A few businesses simply use a brochure style site to showcase what they offer, but most businesses now sell online. If you wish to sell goods via a website you will need an e-commerce site that will allow you to have a shopping cart online and process payments. There are further design features that can help different types of business: if your business relies on visual imagery, for example a photography studio, you will need a website that can showcase your work via an online gallery. Remember, your website will showcase your business and it is essential that it looks good so that it markets your organisation effectively.

Once you have an idea of the sort of website you require you can begin to look at the actual design of the website.

Website designers

It is important that you choose an experienced designer who is able to offer you a professional service and an excellent end product. When choosing a designer you should investigate a number of different options and get quotes before making a decision. Things you should consider when choosing a designer include:

- Their style of working. Look at other websites that they have designed.

- Whether they can do the graphic work as well as the programming. If not, do they work alongside a graphic designer who can provide the graphics?

- How they work with you to plan a website. You are paying for a service and you should expect them to spend time with you getting to know about your business so that they fully understand what you hope to achieve through your site.

- Their knowledge of SEO (search engine optimisation).

- Cost of maintaining your site. If you want to change information on the site how much will this be? Will you have access to the site so that you can change things yourself?

- Check that you will own the copyright to the site once it is completed.

- How long have they been in business?

- Feedback and testimonials from previous clients about their work.

Sadie Knight is a web designer and owns www.glassraven.com.

'Since we became established in 2002, we have worked with quite a few companies whose previous web designer had ceased trading. They were left with either an unfinished site or a site they couldn't change and maintain. Whilst length of trading cannot totally prevent any problems, your designer should be able to tell you what would happen if they were unable to complete designing or supporting your website.'

Domain names and hosting

You will need to buy a domain name and hosting for your business. Sometimes the domain name that you want may already be in use. Check online at a site like www.freeparking.co.uk to see what domain names are available.

For a UK-based business, ensure that your website is hosted in the UK as this will not only help with the speed but it also ensures that your website will be ranked in the UK search engines.

Sadie advises, 'When choosing your domain name remember that it will need to be typed into the computer, so try not to make it too lengthy. Bear in mind common misspellings or different ways that you can write a word with the same sound (eg: reel, real). The most commonly used extensions for a UK-based business are .com and .co.uk and I would recommend purchasing both if available. If not, check that the person who has registered it is not a competitor as you could be accused of 'passing off' or risk losing business if people type the wrong extension. If you purchase a domain with a hyphen, if possible, purchase the non-hyphenated version too. This protects your brand. I have seen clients enter expensive legal battles to try and prevent people from trading on other versions of their domain. Since domain names are not that expensive it is worth protecting your business and brand from the start.'

Creating an effective site

The quality of your website will reflect on your business. You should therefore make sure that it projects a professional image and that information can be quickly and easily accessed. You will need to check your website thoroughly for spelling and grammatical errors. Use a professional copywriter as typos could put off potential customers. Presenting your goods well through your website will help to market your business as a professional organisation who pay attention to detail.

Think about what you hope the website will achieve. Are you hoping:

- To increase sales?

- To generate repeat visitors by offering a discount?

- To use the website to make announcements?

- Or to improve customer service?

Take some time to survey your current clients and find out what they would hope to achieve through visiting your website. Sometimes your expectations and your clients' needs can be very different and so their views can help to make sure that you spend your time in a valuable way. Ask your clients what they hope to achieve by visiting your website and what would encourage them to return to your site. You should always make sure that your approach is user-centred so that your website meets your clients' needs.

Sadie advises, 'An easy-to-use navigation area is an essential part of your website, now that the customer is on your website you want them to stay there. Don't confuse them, make it easy to find the information on your site and guide them through. Ideally, the navigation should be in a consistent location on each page.'

Take some time to think about the content of your website. What would you like to know if you were to purchase your product or service? Break the content down into headings and consider whether you need to include any of the following headings on your website:

- About Us – a section to include information about the history of the company and the staff who are employed. This would allow you the opportunity to emphasise the level of experience that you have within your industry and to highlight any specialisms that you and your team may have.

- FAQ – a frequently asked questions section can help users to find the answers to questions that they may have more quickly. It can also reduce the amount of time staff spend via email or telephone answering these questions.

- Contact Us – this is a legal requirement, but also makes it easier for prospective clients to quickly find a method of contacting you. You should include email addresses, telephone numbers, landline addresses and possibly an online contact form as well. Your contact details should be in a prominent place on your website to help build trust with your prospective client. This is particularly important for e-commerce websites, where you are selling directly online, as it reassures them that you are contactable if there are any questions or problems.

- Services – you may wish to outline your services across a number of different pages, depending on what you offer. For example, a beauty therapist may wish to dedicate one page to massage, another page to beauty treatments and a third page to nails. This also helps with targeting your website in the search engines.

- In The News – if you want visitors to keep coming back to your website you need to update your content on a regular basis. You may choose to have a section to publish information about news within your business and you may also wish to cover any national stories that are relevant, at the time, to your service.

'An easy-to-use navigation area is an essential part of your website, now that the customer is on your website you want them to stay there.'

Sadie Knight www. glassraven.com

- Special Offers – if you hope to use the website to generate sales you may want to consider having a section for special online offers.

- Fees – you may wish to have a page to outline your fee structure.

- Blogs – you can link your blog to your website or make it an integral part of the site. For in-depth information about blogs and how they can help to promote your business, please see chapter 8.

- Terms and Conditions – if you are selling over the Internet you must have fair terms and conditions for your buyer to view. This should include information around postage costs, returns and what the customer should do if dissatisfied.

- Links – do you want to link to other services that complement what you do? For example, a vets practice may wish to link to a grooming parlour, a pet food store or a pet cemetery. If you are going to link with other businesses it is important that you are sure they offer a reputable business that you would want to be associated with.

Sadie Knight advises that it is essential to keep your website content up to date, she says, 'Out-of-date information can reduce the trust your potential clients have in your website. If you did not create your website yourself and there are any areas of your website that you would like to update on a regular basis then consider having a content managed website. It can save you money in the long term as you will require less website maintenance by your designer.'

Legalities

You also need to be aware that there are legal considerations to take into place when designing a website. Legally, companies in the UK must state their company registration number clearly on their site, the place of registration and a registered office address. If the company is being wound up this also needs to be placed on the website.

It is important to have a privacy policy in line with the Data Protection Act and only collect information that is needed from your customer online. Customers need to be aware of any information that you will collect and this information should be kept securely. You should only share information with consent, you can find out more about this by visiting the Information Commissioner's Office website at www.ico.gov.uk. The bottom of every page on your website is an excellent place to put the information that is legally required.

Search engine optimisation (SEO)

It is vital for your business that your website is easily found by potential customers. Search Engine Optimisation, or SEO as it is more commonly referred to, helps search engines to find your site and increase its ranking. SEO is an inexpensive way of helping you to get more visitors to your website and is vital for online marketing, there is little point having a website if nobody can find it.

Lindsey Columbell, Director and Founder of Bojangle Communications, has some advice to improve your website's rankings. 'Spend time researching keywords and key phrases. This is the most important step when building a website that is search-engine friendly. Don't rely on the words/phrases that you think your target audience would search for to find a company like yours, remove the guesswork and find out exactly what is being searched for.'

When choosing keywords and phrases you should be as specific as possible. Lindsey recommends using Google Adwords.

Sometimes it is tempting to cram as many keywords as possible into one page, however, this can complicate the job for the robots that the search engines send out. Lindsey advises, 'Try and write a minimum of 250 words per page, but remember it is important to be succinct and to use real sentences that make sense when reading rather than throwing in key phrases that don't flow well. Leave the information that you have written for a day or so and then revisit it. Does it make sense and flow well?'

If you struggle with your website content it is well worth calling in a professional copywriter with SEO expertise rather than relying on staff who are less sure what to do.

It is good practice to have one page of your website for each different topic. For each topic you can then concentrate on including up to five keywords and phrases. Lindsey advises, 'Keyword stuffing is a no-no. This is when keywords are used indiscriminately in an attempt to improve a website's ranking. Also don't

'SEO helps search engines to find your site and increase its ranking.'

try to hide text, behind images or in the same colour as the page's background. If the search engines work out what you are doing they will penalise you and it could take a long time to get back to the level that you were ranked at!'

It is a good idea to place your keywords in prominent positions, the higher the keyword or phrase appears on the page, the better. Lindsey suggests using keywords and phrases in the following places:

- Page titles.

- Introductory paragraphs.

- Page headings.

- Sub-headings.

- Metadata that is included in the HTML code.

It is important to monitor your SEO so that you can make sure that it is working. Google Analytics is a free tool that will provide you with statistics on the number of visitors that your website has, what pages they visit and what pages they leave the site from. Lindsey says, 'Tracking what keywords your visitors use to arrive at your site can be useful. Also looking at the percentage of people who arrive at your site and leave before looking at another page can lead you to explore why this may be happening and what you can do to encourage visitors to stay longer.'

Google Webmaster Tools is another free tool provided by Google. It helps you to track any errors on your website and ensure that your pages have unique content. You can also view who is linking to your website and keep an eye on your website's presence in Google (position, search volume, click through rate by keyword).

Sadie summarises, 'Analytics and Webmaster Tools are both excellent free pieces of software that give you real insight into what your customers are doing on your website, and can help you to tailor your website to become even more successful.' Sadie has produced an online guide to SEO that can be found at www.glassraven.com/articles/SEO.pdf

Writing for the web

The Internet has opened up a host of opportunities for you to have writing published about your business, from forum posts to blogging. Build regular article writing and promotion into your online marketing strategy. Outsource this if necessary.

When writing online content you need to be aware that it is very different to writing content for print. Research has shown that people read material online much more slowly than in print. Reading from a screen is much more difficult than reading from a book, for example. Usually, visitors to websites are looking to find information quickly and easily. Follow these simple rules to help you to write content for your website more effectively:

- Ask yourself who you are writing for and what they will hope to read.

- Make it clear what each page is about, use headings and sub-headings.

- Don't overcomplicate things, keep language simple and avoid using abbreviations and acronyms that may confuse people. Bear in mind your target audience – if you are targeting a single sector who will search for and understand the acronyms or technical terms you are using, then it would be appropriate and advisable to use them. However, if you are targeting a wider audience you need to adjust the copy to allow for this.

- Avoid underlining text. Most default browser settings will underline a link and this can cause confusion to your reader. Instead of underlining text, you can emphasise sections in bold.

- Be aware that writing words using only capital letters gives the impression that you are shouting at your reader.

- Check that your grammar and spelling are correct. Inaccuracies can lead people to view your website as unprofessional and reflect badly on your business.

- Make sentences short and to the point.

- Use paragraphs and try to use one idea per paragraph so that the information remains clear and concise. The first sentence of each paragraph should give the reader an idea of what the paragraph will cover so that they know whether it is relevant to their needs and worth reading.

'Don't overcomplicate things, keep language simple and avoid using abbreviations and acronyms that may confuse people.'

- Avoid long blocks of text. Break the text up using headings and sub-headings, remember readers are looking to find information quickly and efficiently. If you need to include lengthy pieces of information consider adding in another link that visitors can click if they do want to read more. Keep the most important information 'above the fold' that is in the part of the website that is immediately viewable when the person clicks onto the page. Bear in mind that different screen sizes show different amounts of information.

- Avoid using the past tense as it makes the content of the site appear old and dated.

If you find writing challenging, you could employ somebody to write the content for you. Don't undervalue the importance of good content for your website. It is marketing your business 24 hours a day, 7 days a week so it is important that it is creating the right image to your potential customers.

Remember, your website content is not only targeting your potential customers but also the search engines. It needs to read well for both in order to be successful.

Copyright

It is important that you are aware of copyright issues and how they impact on your business, particularly when publishing information, text and images online.

Since 1st April 1989 it is presumed that all work was copyrighted even if it does not carry the copyright sign. Assume that everything that you read and look at online is copyrighted unless it states otherwise. Also, be aware that photographs are copyrighted. If you want to include photographs on your website you should buy photographs online from a source such as www. istockphoto.com or have your own photographs taken.

If you use a piece of text from somebody else's site and credit it to them you are still breaking the law if you haven't actually received permission.

Summing Up

A website is a great tool for promoting and marketing your business. It can promote your business while you are sleeping and can save you time and money. A website that has been well designed and thought out will help you to strengthen your business's identity. Having a website can also allow you to take advantage of online directories by submitting your site. The Internet is far-reaching and can help you to get your business details broadcast far and wide.

It is important that your website meets the needs of your potential clients. Its design should mean that information is easily accessible. Surveying your customers is a good way to find out what they want from your website and whether it meets their needs.

If you don't have a website, you need to consider that your competitors may have one. Potential customers could be lost if they find your competitor's site.

Quick action checklist:

▪ Have you planned your website content?

▪ Do you need to update your website? It is important that your website is regularly maintained and information is updated to encourage visitors to return.

▪ Have you considered SEO? Is your website reaching as wide an audience as possible?

Chapter Six

Start Marketing Online

Promoting your website though Internet marketing

Once you have a website, it is vital to get the word out. You can have the best products or services in the world, but without constant and ongoing online marketing, a website is unlikely to succeed. In the previous chapter we looked at some elements of search engine optimisation. Now you can learn more about how regular online marketing can help you find customers. Read on for more ideas on how to attract visitors through online marketing, site design and search engine optimisation (SEO).

Site design for promotion

In the previous chapter we looked at some of the basics that will make your website attract visitors. Once people are on your site, it is an essential part of online marketing to consider how you will 'convert' your visitor into someone you can contact on a regular basis to develop a relationship with and lead to making a purchase.

In order to do this, you need to make sure that you have a range of ways to attract people to your site, plus some great ways to make them take action once they arrive there. First, we'll take one more look at your business website: get that right to make the most of any marketing you do.

'You can have the best products or services in the world, but without constant and ongoing online marketing, a website is unlikely to succeed.'

Landing pages

To make the most of any marketing campaign, you should create a landing page which is specifically designed for people visiting the site as a result of the campaign. This page will be written with the marketing campaign in mind, so that the copy on the landing page is attuned to the particular promise or offer that you are making, or the problem that you are offering to solve. The copy should attempt to empathise with the state of mind of the person as they arrive on the site. Devise the content so it gradually draws them towards the action you want to take.

If you have an online marketing campaign it is easy to make your adverts or promotions point to a specific page on your main site. If you are running a print campaign you may want to use a simple code or word at the end of your main web address: this will both ensure that people go to the correct landing page and will also give you an idea of how many people are arriving from a specific promotion. For example, if you want to run a regular promotion for your clothing company's menswear range with the Daily Telegraph, you could direct people who see your advertisement to visit www.yourcompany.co.uk/dt, which would link them to the menswear landing page.

You can test the effectiveness of different content on the landing page by measuring how many people sign up for a newsletter, buy something or take another action that you have planned as an outcome for the marketing. Measure the number of visitors to the page, and the number that take action to calculate your conversion rate.

Conversion rates

The proportion of visitors who take the desired action when they come onto a page on your website.

Example: If 100 people visit your site and 3 sign up for your newsletter, you have a conversion rate of 3%.

(Number of people who take action ÷ Number of people visiting the page x 100 = Conversion rate.)

Approaches to consider for your landing page

Squeeze pages

A squeeze page is a highly targeted page created to gather email addresses from visitors. It is low on distractions – it won't include a menu of links to other pages (known as exit hyperlinks), for example. It will use a range of strategies to make as many people as possible share their email address, usually in return for some free content material.

The copy will be written in order to entice people to take action, and keywords will be included to ensure that the page is picked up by search engines. Use of colour, page design and different button designs should be tested to maximise the effectiveness of the page.

Sales pages

A sales page is a similarly well-focused page, but with the aim of making a sale rather than collecting an email address from a visitor. More and more people are using video and audio to improve the conversion rates of sales pages and squeeze pages.

Sign up boxes and incentives

Whether you opt to send people to your main website, a specific landing page or a squeeze page or sales page, you need to ensure that you have a good way to get people to share their email address with you. In chapter 2 you learned about product funnels. At the top of your product funnel you need to have something free (or very low cost) to entice people to share their contact details with you: your landing page or squeeze page is the perfect place to showcase this offer. You'll need to create a sign up box so people can fill in their contact details to get the incentive. Read on to find out about how to do this in the section on email newsletters, overleaf.

Email newsletters

Spend time building your email contact lists: this is a valuable way to develop relationships with people who will become great loyal customers. You need an ongoing programme of activities to add people to your list.

Make sure that your company stays in touch with people on your list on a regular basis as this can almost double the number of purchases they make.

To find people to go on your mailing list, use a range of techniques. Have a sign up box on your site. Offer a free download, e-course or discount to get people to sign up. Place competitions on other sites to get people to enter and give you their contact details. There are lots more ideas on how to attract people to your site coming up in this and the next two chapters.

'You are not allowed to gather email addresses without the owner's permission, so people need to 'opt in' to receive email communications from you.'

Legalities of building your list

You are not allowed to gather email addresses without the owner's permission, so people need to 'opt-in' to receive email communications from you. Jo Tall of Off To See My Lawyer.Com explains how to collect email addresses legally and use them for marketing:

'Under the Data Protection Act 1998 (DPA) customers are entitled to know if you collect and process their personal details and if you will be sharing them with third parties or sending them outside the European Economic Area. Email addresses count as 'personal data' if it is possible to identify a living individual from them. This means you need to comply with the DPA and can only collect them either:

▓ Directly – by asking customers to register their names and addresses for newsletters etc and getting them to 'opt-in' to receiving marketing materials from you and selected third parties. This involves them ticking a box which will say something like 'By ticking this box, I agree to your Privacy Policy and the activities detailed in it'.

▓ Indirectly – under the so-called 'soft opt-in'. This applies if a person has enquired about your services or bought something from your business and your communication to them relates to similar products or services. In other words you are allowed to assume they consent until they tell you otherwise.

You should, in any case, give your customers/readers the option of unsubscribing from your newsletter/mailshot in every newsletter/mailshot that you send to them.

In addition, you need to have a Privacy Policy displayed on your website (ideally as a link on every page) and especially at the point where you collect any personal data. This will set out what you do with personal data including any future uses you intend to make of the data. Do make sure you really stick to it and don't decide to sell your list to someone else or use it for a completely different purpose. You could face a serious fine! You can get guidance on this from the Information Commissioner's Office (See: www.ico.gov.uk)and also buy ready-made templates of Privacy Policies. The law is very complex and this is just a summary of the key provisions, so please do get legal advice.'

How to use email marketing

Use email marketing to build relationships with existing and potential clients or customers. Make the most of psychological understanding and tactics to warm them up to your business and ensure that you are sending them information that meets their needs. In this way you can bring people closer to purchasing.

Unless you have business finances to create your own email marketing system, you should choose an email service provider, such as Aweber, Mailchimp, Vertical Response or Constant Contact. Alternatively, some shopping carts and websites come with newsletter functionality built in: check that this can do everything you need as some services can be very basic, while others, like 1ShoppingCart are so comprehensive it can be confusing.

How to compare email service providers:

Erica Douglas of social media training provider, AceInspire, advises, 'When picking an email service provider make sure you compare:

- Price – some providers charge per subscriber, others per email sent. Some offer free trials too.

- Delivery rates – what percentage of emails get through to recipients' inboxes and what percentage end up in the junk mail or spam folder.

- What functions it has. Do you need newsletter templates, the ability to run surveys, to link it into your cart, or to offer autoresponders or digital products?
- Reliability.
- Ease of use.
- Support/Customer service.'

Find out more about email service providers at www.aceinspire.com/newsletter-providers/

Planning your newsletter

Once you have picked your newsletter provider, spend some time exploring the templates they offer. You can simply pick one, or customise it. Ensure that your business colours and branding are reflected in the newsletter.

It is better to send out a short newsletter every fortnight or month than spend ages on one newsletter and not get back in touch with people for a year. Think of 12 reasons to get in touch with your customers and potential customers and write one in your marketing plan each month to remind you to mail your customers. Tie this in with other marketing activities, PR and advertising. Make sure you send people on your mailing list an exclusive offer or special discount regularly. This is one way to start building relationships with new and potential customers and to keep them coming back.

'Make sure you send people on your mailing list an exclusive offer or special discount regularly.'

eNewsletter ideas

Are you using:

- eBlasts? Quick offers or snippets of information in-between your main newsletters.
- Email signatures? Get all your staff to have 'sign up for our newsletter' in the signature every time they send an email.
- eNewsletters? Regular news and offers sent out weekly, fortnightly, monthly – you choose!
- eVouchers? Special discounts for subscribers.

There are different styles of newsletter that you can create. Think about what will work best for your type of business and test out what will get the best results. You could opt for:

- A long sales letter. This approach looks at how the potential purchaser is now, outlines their problems, empathises with their feelings and, over a couple of thousand words, sells the solution that your business is offering. It is good for selling to a focused group of people who you know have a particular problem to solve. Don't send this sort of mailing as your regular weekly newsletter.

- An eBlast. This contains one single offer or idea and is an effective way to get people to take action.

- A magazine style newsletter. This contains several short articles, details of news, events and products. Great for updating your customers and keeping them warm to your business, but will have a lower conversion to sales than a long sales letter or short focused offer.

Focus on the results you want for your newsletter and work out a pattern so that you send out regular newsletters with relevant information for your customers and potential customers, interspersed with focused and time-limited special offers to encourage them to buy.

eCourses and eBooks for promoting your business

eCourses and eBooks are useful tools to help you promote your business. An eCourse is a simple set of instructional emails which are written and then set up on an autoresponder, a piece of software that can send out messages automatically to anyone who signs up. Aweber is the best know autoresponder.

An eBook is a great way to showcase your business: if customers or clients need to solve a particular problem an eBook can showcase how your business can help by covering simple self-help tips and practical solutions to the problem.

Why create an eCourse or eBook?

An eCourse, once written, offers a great way to engage with potential customers. Both are relatively low cost to produce: allow a budget for great content, and some design work, but once the book or course is created you can distribute it electronically without further cost. It makes a great 'freebie' or sign up incentive for your company's website. An eCourse has the added advantage that it goes out to someone regularly which will help them develop trust in your business and get a clearer understanding of how you can help them.

Promotion through SEO

Marketing your business over the Internet is the fastest growing way to reach new customers and one that you can't afford to miss out on. Make the most of Internet marketing to find new fans and see your business grow. Search engine optimisation means that you focus on getting your website found by people using search engines like Google for particular keywords and phrases.

Develop a clear list of keywords and phrases to help you promote your business – see chapter 5 for more. Then think about all the different places online that you can use these keywords to link to your business and draw in potential customers searching on those terms.

Seven ideas for online promotion

Think about the activities in the following list and consider which ones could work for your business, then add them into your marketing plan. The key to Internet marketing is little and often, so build time into your diary to carry out your chosen activities on a regular basis:

- Articles – write and place articles on other sites with links back to your site. There are lots of sites which take articles – ezinearticles.com is one of the best known. Look at the rules for each site as there will be guidelines about the number of links you can have in an article, the length of articles and so on. Some article sites focus on particular sectors or topics. The point of publishing articles is to build links back to your main site using your key phrases. Focus each article and use the link so it takes readers back to the most relevant page, not just the front page of your site.

- Blogging – regular entries can help with SEO as well as provide interesting content for readers. There is more about using your keywords in blogging in chapter 8.

- Images – use your keywords when describing images on your main website and blog. Using good descriptions can mean that you come up top of a search on Google Images when you are struggling to appear on the first page for the same terms on the main Google search page.

- Podcasting – use sound recordings to interest a different group of people. Some people react well to the written word while others like to be able to download podcasts and listen to them later. You may find you have sound recording software on your computer already, but there is plenty on offer for a reasonable price. Editing software like Audacity can help you improve your podcasts. Record interviews with experts on topics that will address the needs of your potential clients – the experts can be external to your company or you might want to showcase in-house expertise. Use focused keywords in the title and description for your podcast and include a strong call to action at the end.

- Vodcasting – video is an additional element to add interest and you can use your keywords in the video description. More and more sites are using video as a way to bring clients in. If you are creating videos in-house, acquire software like Camtasia to allow you to edit videos and add text. Put regular videos about your business on YouTube to place the company in front of a whole new audience. Focus on solving problems for viewers and showcasing experts to build trust in your business. Add a call to action at the end of every video so viewers know where to go to find out more, sign up or buy.

- Pay per click advertisements (PPC). You can book adverts through schemes like Google Adwords and pay for your advert to appear when people search on certain key phrases. The more defined your phrase the better results you will get. On a very simple level, if you want to sell handmade candles you need to place adverts that appear on phrases including the words 'buy handmade candles' rather than 'make handmade candles'. If you can bring in further information about your niche, even better: 'buy handmade soy candles' for example. Adwords can be used in ongoing marketing but are very useful for getting your business seen in places you can't reach with SEO (such as other websites that run Google Ads) or before SEO gets results.

- Link building – this is simply approaching other complementary businesses to ask them to link back to your site. While this used to be a key way to help a site rise up search engine rankings, other factors now play an important part and you can find your site is penalised if most of the links in are reciprocal, i.e., 'I'll link to you if you link to me'. Instead, build links by writing guest features for other websites, through Twitter, Facebook and other social media, as discussed in chapter 7.

Summing Up

The Internet gives any business owner or marketer unlimited scope for promotion. It can seem overwhelming at first, so take the actions from this chapter and work through them one by one. Get your website in order first, so you have great pages to draw in new visitors, strongly focused on the issue that you can help them with.

Look at how you will communicate with customers and potential clients on a regular basis with a newsletter. Think about how best to encourage people to sign up to hear from you, and remember to check the legalities of building your list. Could eBooks or eCourses be a way to share valuable information with new contacts and build their trust in your business?

And then make sure you develop a list of online marketing activity that you can do on a regular basis as part of your general marketing plan. There have been lots of ideas in this chapter, and there are many more to come in following chapters where you can learn about social media and blogging.

Quick action checklist:

- Where on your website do you direct people from marketing? Should you create a landing page?
- Do you have a newsletter already? If not, make plans to start one.
- Is there a sign up box on your website? If not, create one as a priority.
- Do you have sign up incentives to grow your contacts database? If not, what could you offer?
- How do you encourage people to sign up and subscribe? Choose a selection of ways to do this from this chapter and build them into your plan.
- Could eBooks or eCourses be a useful way to add value for potential customers and encourage them to share their details with you?
- Which other ways can you use your keywords to build links back to relevant pages on your website?

Chapter Seven
Social Media for Promotion

Social media describes a range of ways to link up with people online. Twitter, blogs and Facebook are all examples of social media, also known as 'web 2.0'. Social media differs from 'traditional' websites as the content is created by its users who have online conversations and build networks. It is ideal for marketing because anyone can create messages and share them with contacts, but you need to know how to use it correctly to market your business.

These sites are key tools that will help you reach many more people and spread your business message.

Why use social media

Social media is a critical tool for almost every business that allows you to build your business's followers and engage with loyal fans. As social media expert Erica Douglas explains, 'There's a theory proposed by Wired magazine's senior editor, Kevin Kelly, that for a creator to be successful you only need 1,000 true fans. That is one thousand people that buy your work, employ your services, read your blog, and retweet your tweets. Once you reach this kind of number you will experience a 'tipping point', where you find that your fans begin to spread your marketing messages for you.' Engaging with real people and getting them to spread your messages is cost-effective and can reach new potential customers in an efficient way. The users you find on social media will be web savvy and used to tweeting or sharing things that they like. People tend to have followers who are similar to them, so your message is getting

'Twitter, blogs and Facebook are all examples of social media.'

to people who are likely to be in your target audience. What's more, people tend to believe messages that come from other 'real people' more than those spread by marketing departments, so 'true fans' can be invaluable.

Read more about the one thousand true fans theory here: http://tinyurl.com/1000true

Twitter

When the phrase 'social media' is used, many people's first thought is Twitter. Twitter was created in 2006 as a way of sharing short messages with a group of people. Now there are millions of users who tweet messages of up to 140 characters every day about their work and life. It is an excellent way to build a network and share interesting and relevant material via links posted as part of your messages.

Erica Douglas says, 'Twitter can be difficult to describe. Some say that it's like 'micro-blogging' as you write one line updates on what you are doing. The 140 character limit for tweets makes it feel like texting and the atmosphere is like a coffee shop - drop in/drop out.'

Twitter is especially popular with bloggers and businesses, so consider if your target audience might be using it. Ask them if you are unsure, as part of your market research.

Setting up a Twitter account for your business

If you have yet to find Twitter, go to www.twitter.com to sign up for a Twitter account and upload a photo. Think carefully about the user name you choose. Will you be using one Twitter account for the business, or in the future can you foresee people being able to get in touch with your customer services department and your PR department via Twitter? In this case you may need to plan for several accounts.

Make sure you have a photograph for your Twitter account. Without a photo people may assume you're a spammer. A business logo is one idea for the image to use on your account, but ring the changes with product shots, images of what is going on at your business etc.

Getting started

Take your first steps by following other people who have a similar area of interest to your business and/or your target audience. Lots of people follow competitors, and then click to see who else is following their competitors and follow them too. To find people with a particular interest simply type something into the search box. A company that sells breast pumps might, for example, search on 'breastfeeding'. To follow someone simply click on the 'follow' button on their profile page. Click on 'followers' to see people who are following them.

Book time to log in every day in your first few weeks on Twitter. Spend just 15 minutes sending a message and finding 10 or 20 more people to follow. People tend to follow back if you follow them so in this way you can start to build your following.

Look up any business contacts you know on Twitter. Retweet their messages alongside your own content. Lots of people follow celebrities too: find relevant ones to your sector that your clients or customers will like and admire.

Erica Douglas advises, 'When you are getting started, write a tweet introducing yourself and saying that you're new to Twitter, engage in conversation with anyone who responds and take it from there.'

What to tweet

Twitter is a great way to promote your business, but if you want to gain a strong following then a blend of tweets is required. Erica Douglas explains the different types of tweets you can use.

- Personal Tweets: How personal is up to you, but an example might be 'weather's great, work's finished, time to fire up the barbie'. Don't share anything that you wouldn't want the world to know. Do consider if yours is the sort of business that people will want to develop a personal relationship with. These tweets have no other purpose than to demonstrate your human side, but they are essential if you want to also promote your business as well.

- Conversation starting tweets: Use questions as a great way to initiate conversations. For example, if you're in the cake making business you might tweet, 'What's your favourite cake flavour?'. These tweets build your

'When you are getting started, write a tweet introducing yourself and saying that you're new to Twitter, engage in conversation with anyone who responds and take it from there.'

Erica Douglas, Social Media Expert.

engagement with your followers. Once someone has engaged with you they're more likely to buy from you and spread your message. It's also handy when it comes to doing market research as you can slip in questions and nobody thinks it's odd!

- Entertaining tweets: For example, a link to a funny photo or video. These tweets give value to your followers and build your audience. It also lightens the mood if you're doing quite a bit of promotion too.

- Tweets that promote someone else's work: This can be retweeting someone else's promotional tweet, or just promoting someone else's blog post/ competition/sale etc. These tweets demonstrate your commitment to your community or niche, they also build up 'favour points' so that when you need something retweeted or you have an event on people will be more forthcoming to help you promote.

- Business tweets: For example, 'Check out my new range of oojywotsits'. These tweets raise awareness of your business, build your profile and help you make sales. These need to be mixed in with all the other types of Tweets.

Erica concludes, 'Don't overthink it, just go with a flow using a blend of the type of message above.'

Twitter to market your business

Once you understand the basics of Twitter and have started to build a following, you can create a plan and start to promote your business. Twitter is great because it is another way to build relationships, and relationships help people to know you, to trust you and to buy from you whether you run a tiny business or have your sights set on growing an international enterprise. It allows you to respond rapidly to people's enquiries, find those who want to know about what you offer and spread the word about sales and promotions.

Tweets for business

Tweets for business can cover topics including:

- New articles on your blog.
- New products.
- How to sign up for your newsletter.
- Useful resources targeted at your customers.
- Special offers e.g. 'Today only – get 50% off our entire Autumn range'.
- Limited availability e.g. 'We're running short on the diary cover in black: order today if you want one'.
- Countdowns e.g. 'Just 3 days left for this month's offer'.

The way to make Twitter work for you is to have a strategy that ties in with your whole marketing plan. Look at the other promotions and offers that you will be running this year, your new product launches and services that you want to promote. Then, plan your month's Twiitter activities around that promotion. Use a service like SocialOomph.com to schedule in tweets in advance. Try out different times of day and frequency of posts and see what works well for your business.

Social media: Twitter tools

Twitter isn't hard to use, but there are some handy tools to make it much easier. Try:

- Tweetdeck: helps you divide the people you are following into columns – much easier to see at a glance who's saying what. You can add in search columns to make it easier to follow topics of interest to your business. It also allows you to link Twitter up with LinkedIn and Facebook.

- Hootsuite: Does all of the above and allows you to schedule tweets in advance; very helpful if you are planning marketing messages for the month ahead.

- Twitterfeed: A helpful tool to automate linking up Twitter, blogs and Facebook.

- SocialOomph: Allows you to vet followers, send automated replies and schedule tweets in advance.

- Twitbacks: Customise the way your Twitter page appears so that you showcase your business in the space on the left side.

- Twibes: join groups to help you find like-minded tweeters, or start your own group.

Although automation is great, any business using Twitter should ensure that there is a 'real person' monitoring the account on a daily basis, responding to queries and sending out fresh news.

Facebook

'Facebook is ideal for businesses that want to reach consumers.'

If you're using Facebook socially, it is an easy step to turn it into another way people can find out about your business news. Facebook is ideal for businesses that want to reach consumers. It works well for local businesses where customers want to share recommendations. And for business-to-business enterprises it still works well as a place to build a community of clients and make it easy for people to recommend or refer people to your business.

If you think Facebook could work for your business, go to 'groups' and click the 'set up a group' button or click on the link at the bottom of any 'page' to set up a page. A group is ideal if you want to promote a membership organisation or club, while a page is more appropriate for most businesses.

- To set up a page – www.Facebook.com/pages/create.php

- To set up a group – www.Facebook.com/groups/create.php

Once you've entered the details asked for, add some content. If you have a blog use 'Networked Blogs' to add your blog to your page so that the content feeds through automatically.

Send messages about your page to people within your target audience who are close contacts and ask them to highlight it to people they think might be interested. Once you have a few fans of your page, your messages will be seen by them and, more importantly, by their friends who visit their profiles. The word can spread about your business to people who are contacts of your contacts.

Add in the occasional exclusive offer for Facebook fans of your page and people will have even more reason to sign up. Mention it in your newsletter, Use Twitter to tweet out to people about the new Facebook page and ask them to join your group. Ask them to help you find your first 100 followers or 500 followers, or offer a prize draw for those who like your page once you reach your target.

Summing Up

Social media is a great way to extend your marketing activities. It can take time to set up but, compared to many other marketing activities is low cost and effective. Focus on building relationships to start off with Twitter, and add in sales and promotional tweets as you get a better feel for what is and isn't appropriate. Use Facebook too and then consider looking for other social media sites relevant to your target audience. LinkedIn is one of the leading sites for business networking and there are many specialist and niche networks. Try out different social media marketing activities and remember to evaluate what is working for you by checking how many people come to your website via Twitter and Facebook. Look at the 'Where Did You Hear of Us?' responses to see if people start to mention social media. Call in a social media consultant if you need help with a strategic focus for your business use.

Quick action checklist:

- Are you using Twitter already for business? If not, sign up for an account and explore it.

- Start by following 5 or 10 new and relevant people each day.

- Create a programme of interesting tweets tied into your marketing strategy.

- Look at which tweets can be automated, but remember to have someone monitoring the account every day.

- Do you need to create a Facebook page for your business?

- If you have a page already, think of three ways to attract new fans.

- Think of three ways to add value for people who are fans already. Could you include them in a draw, make a special offer or limited discount for this group? Implement one idea each week for the next three weeks.

- How can you use technology to link your social media together and save work? It won't take you long to sign up to 'Twitterfeed', 'Friendfeed' and 'Networked Blogs' to maximise all your social media marketing.

Chapter Eight

Blogs and Marketing

Why blog?

A blog, an online 'journal', is a great way to spread the word about a business. Many companies now have blogs. There are lots of good reasons to start a blog for your business. You need to consider the different purposes that your blog might fulfill:

- Will you use it to communicate about the day-to-day running of the business?
- Will you share special offers and promotions on the blog?
- Can you showcase staff expertise on the blog?
- Or would you create an internal blog to communicate with staff?

Your blog can help you develop your company reputation and build relationships with existing and potential customers. It is a way to communicate news fast and build a loyal following. Promoting exclusive offers on your blog can help you develop readers that come back on a regular basis. Adding a sign up box to your blog will allow you to grow the list of people interested in receiving your company newsletter. Adding fresh content to your blog several times each week will help your site rank well on search engines: make sure that the content uses the keywords that you are focusing on for your business. (See chapter 5 for more on keywords).

'Promoting exclusive offers on your blog can help you develop readers that come back on a regular basis.'

Your options for a blog

When setting up a blog you need to decide it if will be part of your main website, an integrated blog, or a separate website, a standalone blog. There are pros and cons to each type. Read on to learn more about your options.

WordPress and Blogger are two of the leading blog providers. Expert blogger Erica Douglas explains about Blogger which offers 'standalone' blogs only. 'Blogger blogs are free but are owned by Blogger. They are ideal for beginners with no technical knowledge. Blogger has a step-by-step guide and you'll have a blog in less than fifteen minutes. Blogger allows "anyone" to start a blog. If you can use a mouse and you can follow instructions you can start a blog on Blogger. The disadvantages are that you don't own your blog and you don't have as much choice on how your blog looks. It doesn't often happen, but Blogger can close your blog down at any time if they take a disliking to your content. On Blogger the look of your blog, the bit your readers see, is called a template and you can choose your template from a selection which you are offered during their step-by-step process.'

WordPress has a lot more flexibility than Blogger as Erica Douglas explains, 'You can opt for a free hosted (standalone) blog, as with Blogger via WordPress.com, but you can also download WordPress from WordPress. org and integrate it to your company site, use your business's hosting. It is possible for your webmaster to customise WordPress Themes to fit in with your company branding.' With WordPress.com, the hosting and managing of the software is taken care of for you. WithWordPress.org you need to install the software on your own server or with hosting provided for you by another company. WordPress.com is great if your company is short on technical support or has a small budget for this. It is easy and simple to set up *fast*, with the confidence that all the upgrades will be done for you. WordPress.org is for you if you want total control! You can change the way your site appears and add in all sorts of widgets and plugins. Unless you have a great technical brain you will need to get help with set-up but you get the same easy-to-use control panel and can update the site yourself. It is the best system if you want to monetise your site. Here are some more differences:

WordPress.com Benefits	WordPress.com Cons
▧ Free. ▧ Easier to set-up. ▧ Everything is taken care of: setup, upgrades, spam, backups, security, etc. ▧ Wordpress host your blog on hundreds of servers, so it is unlikely it will crash if the site gets busy. ▧ Posts are backed up automatically. ▧ It is possible to get extra traffic from blogs of the day and tags that are mentioned on the main WordPress site. ▧ Your login is secure (SSL) so no one can get into your account if you use wifi.	▧ You can't adapt your site to fit with company branding or customise the PHP code behind your blog. This restricts you from integrating payment buttons, for example. ▧ You can't upload plugins. ▧ You can't run commercial advertisements unless you opt for WordPress's own Adcontrol programme (if you have 25,000 visitors per month). ▧ Most of these limitations can be removed if you join the VIP programme run by WordPress which is, in their own words, available to 'high profile' blog creators.
WordPress.org Benefits	**WordPress.org Cons**
▧ Ability to upload themes. ▧ Ability to upload plugins. ▧ Complete control to change code.	▧ You need a good web host that can cope with spikes in traffic. ▧ Your company will need more technical support to set up and run this blog. ▧ Your company is responsible for stopping spam, backups and upgrades.

Writing your blog

Once you have a blog set up you need to plan regular updates as part of your marketing communications. If you have a company with different departments it is worth gathering views on what each department could contribute to the blog. You may want updates about delivery time, for example, alongside your marketing. The bulk of any blog needs to be good content that will keep readers coming back for more. If you run a gardening business, for example, seasonal tips and advice on how to use some of your popular products, readers' questions answered and features from high-profile gardeners will combine to create an interesting 'magazine' style blog.

Frequency of posts

'Aim to update at least once a week: three times a week is probably optimum and daily blogs work well too.'

You need to ensure that posts go up reliably: pick a frequency for blog updates that can be maintained. Aim to update at least once a week: three times a week is probably optimum and daily blogs work well too.

Images, video and audio

Ensure that you use attractive images on every post. You can freely use images owned by your company. If you need further images search for an image library like iStock where you can purchase images. Don't be tempted to just copy images from other sites: always ask for permission and link back if you get it. If you have a range of images to show from an event or to showcase a new range you could create a slideshow using a programme like Picasa, Smilebox or Animoto.

Remember to integrate video and audio into the blog: an audio interview with a celeb can be listened to live or downloaded by those who visit your blog, for example. Different people prefer different ways of interacting with your company and audio and video can capture the interest of those would wouldn't read a written post. You can host videos on YouTube where you can create a company channel: this is another good way to find new prospects interested in your company's offering.

Linking

Link from blog posts to your main website product pages and to other posts on your blog: some of your posts will aim to draw readers further into the site. Also include links to other relevant and useful resources. Always credit anything from another website with a link: this is ethical but can also result in other blogs linking back to you.

Promoting your blog

Once you have established the company blog, you need to promote it as you would any website. To get started, make sure that the feed is set up so that readers who read blogs by RSS (really simple syndication) can get your posts direct to their feedreader.

Setting up a feed

If you need to set up a feed yourself Erica Douglas explains how to do it, '"Burning a feed" is the technical term for sharing your content (everything you publish) with your readers.

You do this by setting up an account with Google Feedburner (it's the first result when you search "Google feedburner" in Google). Once you're inside Feedburner it will take you through everything on offer: watch the video tutorials provided. Firstly you should be directed to "burn a feed" and then you'll have the chance to put chicklets (little buttons) on your blog allowing people to subscribe. Sometimes these buttons are built into a site. There will also be an opportunity to offer updates via email, you need to copy the HTML code and paste it into your sidebar – ask your technical expert to show you how to do this for the first time, it's very simple when you know how and will enable you to do other things down the line. A reader then simply signs up via this small form and they will automatically receive a notice when you've published a new post. This is particularly good for non-bloggers who want to read your blog. Finally, spend some time looking around Feedburner, especially the "analyse" and "optimise" sections.'

Getting a good readership for a blog depends on having good content, adding new posts on a regular basis and promoting the blog consistently. If content creation isn't your strong point or becomes too time-consuming, look for a freelance writer with experience of blogging. Build content creation and blog promotion into your marketing plan.

Here are some more ways to promote your company blog that could form part of your plan:

Basic promotion

Make sure that you mention that your company now has a blog in email and print marketing communications. Think of an incentive for visitors, such as a regular draw to get people into the habit of visiting and signing up for email or RSS updates.

Commenting

Making comments on other relevant blogs can draw readers back to your own blog to read and comment. Ensure that the comments you make are relevant and interesting: it will take more than 'nice blog' to interest people!

Joining groups

Look for groups of bloggers who write on the same topic that your company is interested in and see if there is a community to join. Being part of a blogging community can make a big difference to the success of your blog. *Technorati* is a directory of blogs that you can browse and search to get you started.

Digg and StumbleUpon

Once you have blog posts going up regularly, it is worth looking at getting them submitted to sites like Digg and StumbleUpon. These sites are like a directory of recommendations from readers. You can find WordPress plugins that allow a small button to appear alongside each post with links to social media sharing sites.

Facebook and Twitter

You can also add a small button alongside each post to make it easy for readers to 'like' your posts directly onto Facebook or tweet them out via Twitter.

Twitterfeed

Use a site like Twitterfeed to ensure that your company blog posts get tweeted automatically to the company Twitter account.

Reviews and other customer content

You might want to offer customers the chance to review products on your blog or contribute images and videos of your products in use. Content from 'real people' will add to your blog's interest and authenticity, which will help build trust with readers.

'Content from "real people" will add to your blog's interest and authenticity, which will help build trust with readers.'

Competitions

Running a competition on your blog has lots of benefits for your business. It can help you to attract more people to the blog. Pick a prize that will interest people who fit your customer profile. If your business is aimed at mums of pre-schoolers, offer a prize that would suit a pre-schooler, for example. A competition on your blog can help you get more people on your email list. Make sure that in the competition terms and conditions you explain that by entering, people are giving you permission to add them to your list - and provide a way to opt out. Be realistic that some people signing up are just interested in the competition prize. You can spread the word about the competition on your blog via other bloggers, Twitter, Facebook etc.

Competitions won't result in sales straight away, but by gathering email contacts for people who are interested in your products and services, or in the right demographic to be potential customers, you can then start to build a relationship with them. Make sure you start developing a relationship by mailing everyone who entered to let them know the results of the competition as well as posting the results on your blog. This builds trust and is a chance for you to let them know about your next competition, or give them a discount to buy something if they didn't win.

Summing Up

A business blog will allow you to communicate with your target audience. It is a relatively low cost way of sharing messages about your business and will draw people in to find out more about your products and services.

Make sure that you have a good plan for creating regular content for your blog, and incorporate this and blog promotion into your marketing plan.

Consider whether you will be responsible for your blog, whether you can hand this on to a team member or whether you need to outsource to a freelancer or agency.

Quick action checklist:

- If you don't have a blog, check out the options that would be best for your business.

- Think about the purpose of your blog.

- Make a plan for how often you will post and the topics you want to cover.

- Consider who will create the content: yourself, other staff, guest writers or a freelancer.

- Make a plan to promote the blog.

Chapter Nine

Planning and Evaluating

If you have read all through this book, you should be brimming with ideas to help you market your business, and this chapter is all about bringing it all together. Read on to find out how to create a marketing plan, how to determine which activities work well for your business, and where to go for more help and support.

Why you need to plan your marketing

Marketing without a plan is simply using tools at random, without any idea of what is effective for your business. A focused and planned approach will save you time, money and effort. Lindsey Collumbell, Director & Founder of Bojangle Communications, explains, 'Marketing is a key factor in the success of your business. To be successful you need to have established who your customers are, how you reach them, how you win new customers and how you keep existing customers happy. On top of all this you need to constantly review and analyse what you do, to make sure you stay ahead of the competition. An effective marketing plan will cover all of these points and be linked to, and complement, your overall business strategy.'

What your marketing plan will do

Every business needs to make money, and to do this almost every business will need to continually reach more potential customers. Lindsey Collumbell says, 'A successful marketing plan will move those in your target market further up the tree (see overleaf), preferably to the point where they recommend you to others …'

'Marketing without a plan is simply using tools at random, without any idea of what is effective for your business.'

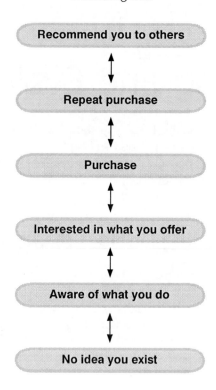

Marketing tree

Recommend you to others

↕

Repeat purchase

↕

Purchase

↕

Interested in what you offer

↕

Aware of what you do

↕

No idea you exist

About your business

In chapter 1 you started to think about your business aims: now is a good time to go back and review those aims. If you are sure and clear about your overall business aims it is much easier to make an accurate and well thought out plan that will help you get closer, step by step.

What are your business aims?

- To build the business profile?
- To find new contacts?
- To make sales?

Note down your business aims here now:

....

....

You also thought about your USP – unique selling point – and UPB – unique perceived benefits. Lindsey Collumbell reminds us, 'Most products and services have unique selling points – a feature, price or other attribute that makes what you do attractive to customers and different to the competition. Once you have established your USP/s your marketing plan will maximise the benefit of them to your target market/s.'

Make some notes here about these important concepts:

- Why should I buy from you?
- What's good about your business?
- What makes it different?
- How will it help me?

Note down what is different and special about your business here now:

....

....

....

Remember, if you find it hard to come up with what is unique about your business, it is time to ask people. See chapters 1 and 2 for more about research with customers.

Your marketing campaign

Now you have a little background to your business firmly fixed in your mind, it is time to think about why you are marketing the business and what you want to achieve.

It is clear that without marketing it is hard to grow a business and attract new customers. It is much easier to market effectively if you are certain about what you want the outcomes to be and you know who your target audience is (see chapter 1 if you are unsure).

Who are you targeting?

Thinking about your target audience, do you have a picture of your ideal customer? Perhaps look at the customers who are loyal repeat visitors, and those clients who spend the most. Bear in mind that you want to attract more of this type of person. If, as suggested in chapter 2, you have been asking people 'where did you hear of us?', has this shown you any trends for where you are finding your most valuable customers? On the converse side, do you have people who are time-wasters? How are they attracted into your business? As Lindsey Collumbell explains, 'You need to know who you want to reach to make sure you don't waste time, money and effort marketing to people who are not interested or relevant to what you do, e.g. if you are a high-end web design company, there is little point aiming your marketing at OAPs! It is well worth finding out so you focus your marketing on attracting great clients rather than those who make your heart sink.'

'It is well worth finding out so you focus your marketing on attracting great clients rather than those who make your heart sink.'

What do you want to promote?

You may want to create a campaign to raise your business profile in general, or you might want a specific campaign which will launch a new product or service.

You could have a campaign that ties into an important season for your business. Shoe and uniform retailers have specific campaigns running up to September and when the children go back to school, for example, and many retailers have specific marketing campaigns in the run-up to Christmas. If you are clear about what you want to promote, it is much easier to succeed. Someone marketing products that make great Christmas gifts would have to start almost right after the previous Christmas to create their plan, source samples, build media contacts and get samples to journalists by July, when many of the monthly glossy magazines are planning their Christmas pages.

Note down here exactly what you want to promote – be as specific as possible:

....

....

....

What action do you want people to take?

Once you know *what* you want to promote, you should also look at the action you need people to take. Lindsey Columbell asks, 'Why are you conducting a marketing campaign? It could be to increase sales, to achieve a certain number of customers, or to generate a certain amount of turnover. It could be to reach a new audience, such as break into the consumer market having successfully established your product/service in the corporate market.'

If you are trying to raise your business profile, one of the strands of your marketing campaign may simply be to get more people to be aware of your business. Or, you might want to get them to take action and sign up on your website to receive your newsletter. Or, you might actually want to get previous customers to the point of purchase of a new product.

Depending on the size of your business, you may simply have one ongoing campaign with promotions within it for different launches, events or services, or you may find it simpler to plan a campaign for each thing that you want to promote. In that way you can build up a series of regular activities that you know work for your business and adapt them to each new launch.

Think carefully about the scope of your planning as it will work better if you know that you are planning a single ongoing campaign for the year *or* focusing your activities on particular launches.

Working out your objectives for your campaign

Once you know who you are targeting and what you want them to do, as well as the overall aims for your marketing, it is time to break things down and work out some specific objectives.

Lindsey Columbell advises, 'Each objective you set needs to be SMART, i.e.

- ▦ Specific – e.g. win ten new customers.

- ▦ Measurable – place a value to check whether the objective is met.

- ▦ Achievable – if you can't achieve the objective don't set it.

- ▦ Realistic – you must have the necessary resources to meet the objective.

- Timely – set a deadline rather than leave the objective open-ended.'

Take the time to check the data your business has on your current numbers of:

- Customers
- Enquiries
- Sales
- Website visitors . . .

These are some starting suggestions – there may be other data that is relevant for you and your business. Note them down here:

....

....

....

....

....

If you don't have the data you need, it is important to start counting now to give yourself a baseline to measure the success of your marketing activities against. Do you need to:

- Look at your website statistics? Does your site have Google Analytics installed or do you have another way to assess the number of unique visitors to your website?
- Count footfall into your premises?
- Ask customer services for the number of enquiries they get, or set up a system to monitor this?
- Ask the sales department for current sales data, or set up systems to regularly count sales?
- Ask everyone who visits, enquires or buys, 'Where did you hear of us?'

Once you understand the current position, you can set some targets, and don't forget to set a timescale for each target. Lindsey Collumbell suggests, 'When creating a marketing plan, it is important to set a timescale. Are you embarking on a short-term, medium-term or long-term marketing campaign? The objectives you set (with measurable targets) need to be relevant and measurable in the timescale you set.'

Note down your targets for each month. These will be affected by factors such as the type of business you have, the seasons, economic climate etc. If you are in a business with different departments you will need to discuss the targets together.

Activities

Are you clear about what you want your marketing campaign to achieve? Now is the time to go back through the book and add in the activities that you are going to do to help your business reach the targets you have set.

Remember to think about including:

- Advertising.
- Business branding.
- Email marketing.
- Events.
- Internet marketing.
- Media relations.
- Networking.
- Promotional materials.
- Sales.
- Sales promotions.
- Social media.
- Telemarketing.

'When creating a marketing plan, it is important to set a timescale. Are you embarking on a short-term, medium-term or long-term marketing campaign?'

Lindsey Collumbell
Director &
Founder, Bojangle
Communications.

Make use of national events and seasons: note these and important business dates into your plan so you can co-ordinate activities.

Plan for the coming year, and have a second file to note down feedback and ideas for the next year. This will make it easier to create your next marketing plan.

Laying out your plan

There are lots of different ways to lay out a marketing plan. Here are some things to think about. Do you find it easier to view printed documents or work from online files? Will you need to share the plan with others? However you create your plan, it is strongly recommended that you have an overview of activities which you can print out and place where everyone can see what is coming up.

Then, make sure that you have a written section which outlines the business aims, your target audience and your marketing targets. Create a section all about the activities you have planned.

Here is an example of a simple activity plan for an optical practice which uses regular business activities and seasonal events to ensure that there is something going on each month. This practice has a computerised system which counts sales and sight tests. These can be analysed weekly or monthly, and the manager can also look at age, gender and location of those visiting the practice.

Now create your plan. Don't forget to include:

- Business aims.
- USP.
- Aims for promotion.
- Target audience.
- Action for people to take.
- Activities.

Month	Events	Themes	Promotional activity	Cost	Target group	Evaluation
Jan	Sale		Window display, Posters, flyer, newsletter, adverts.	£750	Adults	Number of sales frames sold cf last year, number of eye tests booked.
Feb			Window display of fashion frames. Chocolates and voucher for local beauty salon with every order on the 14th. Send press releases and photos in advance to get media coverage.	£800	Women	Media coverage – total reach. Ask customers what brought them to the practice and note down if media coverage effective. Compare number of women visiting the practice to last year's data.
Mar		Easter	Window display, newsletter to local families, holiday coloring competition	£450	Children	Ask whether the newsletter prompted people to book as part of regular question to customers. Number of entries in colouring comp.
Apr	Contact Lens Promo		Letter to potential customers, invite journalist in to try out new contact lens range.	£350	Adults	Ask customers, 'where did you hear of us?' and 'what made you come in today?' and see if letter effective. Note reach of media coverage.
May	Eye Health Week		Stall in shopping centre, talks to local pensioners clubs about the importance of eye tests. Take bookings for eye tests after talks and at the stall. Press release about events.	£350	OAPs	Ask customers, 'where did you hear of us?' and 'what made you come in today?' and see if letter effective. Note reach of media coverage. Compare number of OAPs attending. Look at total spend of new patients compared to time spent on promotion.

Lindsey Collumbell advises, 'Your plan shows what activities you will do and when and puts a corresponding cost to each activity, allowing you to plan your budget and resources accordingly. This way, you can see what you need to do and when in order to meet your overall desired result.'

This action plan opposite is for a baby shop which also has an online store. The owner has decided on a regular pattern of ongoing promotion each month and fills in specific activities.

Implementing your plan

Promoting your business is easy if you break it down into small steps and do a little each day. A simple way to do it is to work on a different activity each week, every month. You could do something like the action plan on page 111:

- Week 1 – PR.
- Week 2 – Advertising.
- Week 3 – Online marketing.
- Week 4 – Offline marketing.

Write this into your plan and set a reminder on your computer each week to remind you what you should be working on.

Top tips for an effective marketing plan.

Here are some tips for an effective marketing plan from Lindsay Columbell:

- Set clear, realistic and measurable objectives.
- Set deadlines for meeting objectives.
- Set a budget for the campaign and schedule activities accordingly.
- Ensure one person is responsible for the plan's execution and delivery.
- Regularly review your progress – learn from your achievements and failures and amend the plan accordingly – your plan shouldn't be set in stone.

April	What	Media	Audience	Cost/Time	Evaluation
Week 1	Press release (Choose a topic for each month).	Local media.	Local mums .	3 hours	Articles, enquiries, sales.
Week 2	Advertising.	Local media .	Local mums .	£125 per month for ad in local parenting magazine 1 hour to set up £75 for designer.	Enquiries, Ssles.
Week 3	Online promotion.	Write and schedule Twitter messages, Write blog posts for the month and create feed into Facebook. Write newsletter and schedule.	Parents' nationally.	$26 for subscription to SocialOomph.	Visits to site, enquiries, sales.
Week 4	Arranging events .	Summer NCT fair Ask for posters, add to next month's newsletter, order in flyers, check stock, create competition.	Local parents .	£25 for stall. 2 days staff time to set up and staff the stall.	Sales on the day, names for mailing list, ongoing sales .

Getting help in

Look at the skills within your business. If you are to carry out a successful marketing campaign you need to be clear about what you can do in-house and where you might need help. Do you have an in-house designer or will you commission an agency or freelancer? Do you have professional copywriting skills or will you need help here too? Should you get help to ensure that the company blog is updated every week, and could a social media professional write more effective tweets for you?

Go through the plan again to flag up where you will need to call in other departments or external help. Will you need to use a public relations agency, a direct mail specialist, an advertising agency, a graphic designer, a social media professional or a printer? All these and more are likely to come into your plan at some point. If you have established relationships with external suppliers, that's great. If not, schedule in time to research, get recommendations and ask for quotes and timescales. Build these into your plan, as it is all too easy to get to the point where you need to start sending promotional materials out and find they are still being printed, for example.

Finding a freelancer

If you need occasional or ongoing help with specific jobs that are outside your expertise, a freelancer might be just what you need. You can book a freelancer to do a one-off job for you or send them work every month. Find freelancers at local networking meetings and by networking through online business fora. Ask for recommendations as this can be a great way to find someone with minimal risk. There are also specific freelance websites where you can post your work and get quotes from a range of freelancers.

To work successfully with a freelancer, be clear about what you need and when you want it delivered. Agree the fee you will pay – usually per hour, but sometimes the freelancer will have a set fee for a job. Make yourself available in case they have queries. Feed back about any amendments you need clearly and promptly, and remember to pay on time if you want to develop a successful continuing relationship with a great freelancer.

Commissioning agencies

Sometimes the work you have may need more than a single freelancer. If you are planning a direct mail or PR or advertising campaign and don't have an in-house team you may want to commission an agency to handle everything for you. Find three relevant agencies and have a chat on the phone about what you need: this way you can be sure that they have the skills and experience you are looking for. Then, ask the agency to prepare a pitch for your business, The agency should come up with ideas and demonstrate how it would carry out your work. Staff may come to your office to pitch, or you might visit them, or you may be able to do this remotely using virtual conferencing software which can allow you to get in high quality specialists regardless of their location.

Evaluation

In chapter 2 you were asked 'can you count where your customers come from?'. Have you built a 'where did you hear of us?' box into your order form, or have you started asking every customer and noting down their answers?

There is little point carrying out promotional activities if you don't evaluate what works. It can lead to you wasting time and effort year after year carrying out activities 'because that's what we always do'. A little investigation can show you where your most profitable customers and clients come from, and allow you to focus your efforts on creating further marketing to these channels.

For each marketing activity, be clear about your objectives and the action you want people to take and then plan how you will evaluate it *before* you start. Work out the cost of the activity too, and as part of the evaluation look at the number of sales made.

For example, if you are carrying out a Twitter campaign, create a specific landing page for that promotion. Note down the number of unique visitors to your website both for the month *before* the campaign starts, and for the same month last year and the year before. Think whether there are any other activities which could also be bringing new visitors to the site and make a note of these. Set the Twitter campaign to run, and then check the site stats once a week to see the number of people coming from Twitter. Count visitors to the

'There is little point carrying out promotional activities if you don't evaluate what works.'

landing page and see where else they go on the site. Are you able to follow these people through and see what action they take? Have they signed up for your newsletter or made a purchase? How do the sign ups and purchases compare to the time and cost involved in creating and running the Twitter campaign?

Cost of creating and running Twitter campaign	£175
Number of site visitors this time last year	3,790
Number of site visitors last month	4,129
Number of direct hits to landing page	1,220
Number of site visitors this month	5,449
Est increase visitors due to campaign	1,220-1,320
Total number of newsletter sign ups from this group	73
Sales directly attributable to visitors from Twitter	£370

You then might look at this as a successful campaign and continue it for another month. You may find that you get fewer people signing up for the newsletter as you are speaking to the same group, and perhaps more sales as you remind them again how you can solve their problems through tweets *and* the newsletter.

Costs	
Staff costs	£1,200
Exhibitor's fee	£6,000
Stand and banners	£900
Pre-show advertising	£3,000
Accommodation and meals	£500
Total costs	£11,600

Similarly, if you run an event look at the costs and time involved. For a show, you'd need to count up, say, two days' staff time in preparation, plus two people to staff the stand for the two days of the event, giving a total of six days.

Then, you need to look at all the leads gathered as a result of the event and track them over time to see how these convert into sales.

If the trade show takes place in January, for example, you might get three good orders at the event, and 20 solid leads. The orders at the event might make it seem like it wasn't worth doing the show as you only take £2,250, but by following up after the show with ongoing marketing it seems much more worthwhile, particularly if you see that a number of firms are placing repeat orders:

Profit from orders by leads from trade show	January – during show	Jan – orders placed after follow-up call	Feb	March	April	May	June	July	August
Smith Bros	£1,000								
Jones & Sons	£500				£500				£500
Merx Co	£750								
Taylor Needham		£3,000					£3,000		
Inspire		£250							
Harold LLP			£750						
Johnson Retail group					£1,000		£10,000		£1,000

By June this company had recouped its investment in the trade show in orders.

Think about how best to evaluate your marketing activities and build this into your plan now. Then go back to your overall aims for your business and marketing and see how the activities you have planned might bring you closer to success.

Summing Up

A marketing plan will set you head and shoulders ahead of any business that is doing its marketing on a reactive basis. Within your plan be clear about your:

■ Business aims.

■ USP.

■ Aims for promotion.

■ Target audience.

■ Action for people to take.

■ Activities.

Work out a regular schedule for your activities and, crucially, how you will know whether they are effective and worthwhile. Factor in time and resources to find external help, as this will allow you to market your business even more effectively.

Quick action checklist:

■ Have you started creating your marketing plan?

■ Do you need to get in external help?

■ Do you have clear plans for evaluating the success of your marketing activities?

Help List

General Information

Information Commissioner's office

Information Commissioner's Office, Wycliffe House, Water Lane, Wilmslow, Cheshire SK9 5AF
Tel: 0303 123 1113
www.ico.gov.uk
An independent authority that upholds information rights. You will find useful information and advice around freedom of information and data protection issues.

Expert advice

Dee Blick

The Marketing Gym, 4 Irwin Drive, Horsham, West Sussex RH12 1NH
Tel: 07845 439332
www.themarketinggym.org
Dee Blick is founder of The Marketing Gym and an award-winning Chartered Marketer. She is also author of *Powerful Marketing On A Shoestring Budget For Small Businesses.*

Erica Douglas

ACEInspire, Channel View, Bexhill, TN40 1JT
Tel: 0845 643 1874
www.aceinspire.com
Erica Douglas is a partner at ACEInspire, which provides flexible and affordable training for businesswomen and social media consultancy.

Jo Tall

c/o Ashdown Hurrey, 20 Havelock Road, Hastings, East Sussex. TN34 1BP
Tel: 020 8946 2355
www.offtoseemylawyer.com
Jo Tall is Director of Off To See My Lawyer.Com, a company that gives
guidance to business owners on legal matters.

Lindsey Collumbell

Bojangle Communications Ltd, 2 Virginia Close, Ashtead, Surrey KT21 2NW
Tel: 01372 274975
www.bojanglecomms.co.uk
Lindsey Collumbell is Director & Founder of Bojangle Communications a
marketing consultancy.

Sadie Knight

Glassraven, South Barn, Trevescan Farm, Sennen, Penzance TR19 7AQ
Tel: 0845 226 26 17
www.glassraven.com
Sadie Knight is Director of Glassraven, a Business Link approved web
designer.

Survey software

Survey Monkey

www.surveymonkey.com
Useful site to support market research and to analyse results.

PR resources

Aweber

www.aweber.com
Low cost eMarketing tool.

Cision

http://uk.cision.com
Newsletter providers.

Constant Contact

www.constantcontact.com
An affordable eMarketing system that also includes a free trial offer.

Journalism.co.uk

www.journalism.co.uk
A useful website where you can get your press release published.

MailChimp

www.mailchimp.com
A tool that helps you to publish and share newsletters.

PR Basics

www.prbasics.co.uk
Free download of Press Release template and other resources to help you with PR.

PR Newswire

www.prnewswire.co.uk
Add your press release to their website.

Response Source

www.responsesource.com
Press release distribution website.

Vertical Response

www.VerticalResponse.com
eMarketing tool that includes a free trial offer.

Professional bodies

IoIC - The Institute of Internal Communication
Suite GA2, Oak House, Woodlands Business Park, Linford Wood, Milton Keynes MK14 6EY
Tel: 01908 313755
www.ioic.org.uk
The UK's leading professional body for in-house, freelance and agency staff involved in internal communications.

Chartered Institute of Marketing
The Chartered Institute of Marketing, Moor Hall, Cookham, Maidenhead, Berkshire SL6 9QH
Tel: 01628 427120
www.cim.co.uk
The world's largest organisation for professional marketers.

Chartered Institute of Public Relations
CIPR Public Relations Centre, 52-53 Russell Square, London, WC1B 4HP
Tel: 020 7631 6900
Email: info@cipr.co.uk
www.cipr.co.uk
The CIPR is a chartered body and membership is on an individual basis.

Design and Art Directors' Association
9 Graphite Square, Vauxhall Walk, London SE11 5EE
Tel: 020 7840 1111
www.dandad.org
D&AD inform, educate and inspire those who work in and around the creative industries.

Institute of Practitioners in Advertising

44 Belgrave Square, London SW1X 8QS
Tel: 020 7235 7020
www.ipa.co.uk
The UK's leading trade and professional body for advertising, media and
marketing communications agencies.

The National Union of Journalists

Headland House, 308-312 Gray's Inn Road, London, WC1X 8DP
Tel: 020 7278 7916
Email: info@nuj.org.uk
www.nuj.org.uk
Maintains a list of freelancers.

Society for Editors and Proofreaders

Riverbank House, 1 Putney Bridge Approach, Fulham, London SW6 3JD
Tel: 020 8785 5617
www.sfep.org.uk
Maintains a list of freelancers

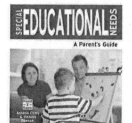    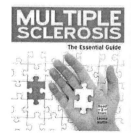